I Still Run In My Dreams

(A Physical and Spiritual Journey Through Quadriplegia)

Written by David Moore
Published by David Moore

COPYRIGHT

COPYRIGHT PAGE

Naturally, the most important feature of a copyright page is the copyright declaration itself. It generally appears in the following order, and includes the author's name and the date of initial publication:

Copyright © 2012 by Author's Name

There are variations, of course. The word "copyright" itself is sometimes eliminated in favor of just the symbol:

© 2012 by Author's Name

Additionally, the copyright page often features a "reservation of rights," which describes whatever permissions are allowed for the use / distribution / reproduction of the work. "All rights reserved" means that no permissions have been granted, and the full statement generally looks something like this:

All rights reserved. No part of this publication may be reproduced, distributed, or transmitted without the express consent of the author.

Other elements of a copyright page may include the following:

Photo and/or design credits

Editor credits

Printing and/or ordering information Edition

ISBN*

* NOTE: ISBN's are available for purchase as part of your self-publishing package here at the NYU Bookstore.

FOREWARD

A special thanks to all of those whose helped make this book possible including the amazing watercolor artist, Maria Barry, who created the artwork for the cover.

Additionally, I want to thank all the amazing doctors, therapists, nurses, and other caregivers that give so much of themselves to help people survive and flourish in whatever condition they are dealt. I had beautiful and loving people that helped me to recover and regain much of my original life. Their efforts enabled me to be where I am today. They helped facilitate a high quality of life that I enjoy and I will be forever grateful to them.

I wrote this book as a way to re-live all the efforts given by all of those caregivers. A way to remember all the struggles I had to go through, as well as learning to laugh under trying circumstances. Writing this book was easy because I was merely telling the story of my life.

I have talked to therapists and other patients in situations similar to mine, and have repeatedly gotten the same answer to a particular question, even from those disabled from birth. When we sleep, we never have dreams where we have limitations. It has been twenty-one years since I became paralyzed, yet I have never had a dream where I was confined to a wheelchair.

In my dreams I can walk, run, and sometimes fly. There are no limitations when I'm asleep. It's always surprised me that my daily struggles are never represented in my dreams. Whatever the purpose, dreams allow me to escape and be free; free from my wheelchair, free from all the accompanying problems. It allows me to feel the breeze in my face as I run across a meadow. If I've learned one thing through all this, it's that there are more important things in life than having the ability to walk. The value of a person lies from the shoulders on up, and not from the shoulders on down.

TABLE OF CONTENTS

I Still Run In My Dreams
(A Physical and Spiritual Journey Through Quadriplegia)

CHAPTER ONE
The Accident

We've all had those moments when the line between the real and the unreal is temporarily blurred. A nap in the afternoon where we wake, not sure if it's day or evening. A noise waking us in the dead of night where we're not sure if the sound was from outside, or merely from our dreams.

I felt my quiet little world suddenly interrupted by the harsh sound of rocks rattling from below. I found myself in that realm between the conscious and unconscious, my mind furiously attempting to define what this new sound was that so unkindly disturbed my slumber. How much time had passed? I had no way of knowing, but with the realization that my car had left the roadway, my eyes flew open and my heart sped. I could see myself already heading down a steep incline, moments from a sloping embankment. There was a vivid picture of an earthen driveway connecting the void of a deep ravine. There was no time to swerve, no time to stop. The car hit the driveway from the side and flew skyward, no longer in contact with solid earth.

I was still processing what was happening, denying it all because to accept would be too harsh of a reality. Funny thing happens when your mind is put into a life threatening moment. My only explanation is that your mind begins processing faster than you ever thought it could, and in so doing the world around you slows down. It's easy to think that when you reach that moment, when your life may end, there would be overwhelming fear. For me, I could only think of survival and what I needed to do to help make that happen.

The car's front rose up flipping end over end, front over back. Like a memory permanently tattooed into my mind I remember tucking and rolling with the car, the chest strap holding my body tight. In a slow and surreal matter of seconds my car flipped three times, each blow crushing the roof down closer around me. Suddenly all motion stopped. A tranquil quietness descended upon my soul and seemingly to the car as well. I knew it had only been seconds. That's what my rational mind was telling me, but the experience made it seem so much longer. I lay upside down in what amounted to a crushed tin can. Unable to move I looked toward my body to assess the damage.

I was the baby, the fifth of five children. The oldest was my brother Dennis, followed by Dianna, Derryl, Debbie, and finally me. I grew up in a family that was stable and loving. My father was a set-up man at International Harvester and my mom ventured into many jobs, but I remember her best for selling Avon. My brothers involved me in many activities growing up and I learned to play many sports. I graduated High School having had a very successful tennis year qualifying for the Illinois State Tournament. I had a couple of scholarship offers and after visiting Marycrest University, decided to play tennis there.

Marycrest had previously been an all girls Catholic school until just a few years earlier. They had a new coach dedicated on comprising a stellar team. The university had three indoor tennis courts, and above the three tennis courts was a pub. Many times I would follow up tennis practice by spending a few more hours upstairs drinking and meeting fellow students, especially girls, which outnumbered the men six to one.

One evening a poster caught my eye advertising a movie that was being shown in a couple days. I didn't recognize the title of the film, but it sounded like a good opportunity to enjoy a night out and (who knows?) maybe meet some new people. I arrived that night and snuggled in with fellow students in a back room. The organizers were handing out bags of popcorn and getting the projector ready to go. The lights dimmed, the screen lit up, and the film began.

I was immediately intrigued when I realized the film dealt with a champion skier. The story was of Jill Kinmont, perhaps the best skier in the U.S. She was in a competition atop a mountain competing for another skiing championship. The conditions were icy and the course was difficult. I cringed when I saw her lose control and go off the side of a cliff. I wondered if she was going to die, but something I considered much worse happened. She was alive, but paralyzed from the neck down.

I was eighteen at the time and knew about the possibilities of paralysis from Spinal Cord damage, but other than that I had no contact with anyone who was paralyzed and knew little of what it entailed. I sat there quietly watching this wonderfully athletic girl reduced to being confined to a wheelchair. This promising skier, perhaps a future Olympic champion, was reduced to a person I couldn't possibly fathom. Someone who couldn't walk, could barely use her hands and arms and who felt a sense of accomplishment when she was able to extract a single potato chip from a bag by flinging her clasped, somewhat lifeless hand inside it. The bag and most of the chips were destroyed, but she proudly brought out one unscathed, nestled softly between her two fingers.

I felt vulnerable. I had spent my life valuing my athletic ability, like my ability to hit a tennis ball or to shoot a basketball. I took for granted those early morning jogs when I would listen to the world wake up around me. The crisp cool air, the birds singing, and the pitter-patter of my running shoes as I cruised down the street. I couldn't take my eyes off the screen, but at the same time I felt almost violated. My heart went out to this young girl. How can this woman possibly be smiling I thought, as she took that chip out of that bag. She's lost everything! Everything that was important is gone! She surely would have been better off had she just died, and now she's trapped to live the rest of her life confined to her own seemingly useless body. I'm sure I wasn't the only one sitting on the floor that night, popcorn in hand, imagining what it would be like to have something like that happen to themselves. I felt nauseous as I contemplated such a scenario. I wouldn't possibly want to go on in such a pathetic state, I thought. I'm sure it would be much better that I die immediately than to be deprived of all the things I held dear. This movie stayed with me. It moved me! I was filled with mixed emotions.

I admired Kinmont's attitude. I was amazed with her drive to make the most of a horrible situation. I was impressed with her ability to make a difference by becoming a teacher when the world as she knew it had crumbled. Yet there was also a bit of, well, a bit of disbelief. Does she fully understand everything she's lost? Did she lose her mind? She can't possibly be happy after all she's been through! I went home that night with a sense of sadness. I knew it could happen to anyone, including me. I was one of the lucky ones though! I woke up early the next morning and went for my morning jog. I never forgot that movie, but over time I rarely thought about it. It wasn't something that would ever happen to me. I was one of the lucky ones, or perhaps more fittingly, she was one of the unlucky ones. How unaware I was of how my feelings would change a mere 14 years later.

I spent my first year of school playing basketball, tennis, drinking alcohol, and meeting girls. Unfortunately, I spent far less time attending class and doing homework. I did happen to make the Dean's list my first semester, but only because good grades were required for me to participate in sports. The second semester was far different. After playing on the basketball team for the beginning of the season, I moved on to the tennis court. After all, that's what I was being paid to play. Most of the players on the team were seasoned partiers and soon I learned to be just as seasoned or perhaps a better word would be krausened. I still drank less than most of them, but that was more because of their excesses than a lack of my own.

I finished the second semester failing three of my four classes and getting a D in the fourth, but my tennis coach did line me up with a job at UPS and I was more than eager to enter the workforce and begin making my share of spending money. I found I was a much better worker than a student, and in two years was promoted into part time management as a Pre-load Supervisor. My hours were a bit hard to get used to. I would wake up at 3AM and be on the road by 3:30. My desire to go out till the early hours of the night made this schedule all the more challenging, but I was still able to hold down the job, do the best work possible and be on time and present. The advantage of such an early morning schedule was the fact that I would be done with work before noon and had the rest of the day to do what I wanted, and that usually meant sports and physical activities.

I had a friend named Randy who, by the way, was the one who recommended me to the coach that gave me the scholarship and ultimately my UPS job. Randy also worked for UPS but he worked in the evening, which allowed us the opportunity to hang out and play basketball or tennis during the afternoon. This was a time when my proficiency in both sports advanced dramatically.

I took classes during this time, sporadically and only part time, but I was able to maintain a grade point average of about 3.5. Weekends were for tennis and local Gus Macker basketball tournaments. We did well in the basketball tournaments, but never won any of them, but the tennis tournaments were a different story. Randy and I won quite a few tournaments during the summer and often met in the finals of the singles. Eventually, I was once again offered a scholarship to play tennis. The coach was amazing and he offered me what amounted to a full ride, and this time from a University ranked in the top ten nationally in NAIA (the National Association of Intercollegiate Athletics).

My time at the university was as memorable as I could have hoped. My grades could have been better, but they were still much better than that wasted semester my freshman year. I qualified for Nationals. I had the best overall record on the team, winning twenty eight times and losing only four. I found myself playing at a higher level than ever before. My first major tournament matched me with a Teaching Pro that would have beat me the year before, but I dispatched him 6-4, 6-0. I eventually lost in the semifinals to a player from the Philippines in a close match.

In the summer of the same year, I played in a tennis tournament in a small river town that was part of a July 4th celebration. I won the singles by beating Randy in the finals and teamed up with Randy to win the doubles. The town was loaded with Independence Day celebrations so I wandered down to the festivities and settled in at the beer tent. I saw the director of the tournament smile and wave me over. I sat down at the table with her. I had seen this girl grow up playing tennis tournaments just as I had. She was an attractive tennis player in High School that my friends and I enjoyed watching. One thing led to another and soon I found myself dating this girl. After a couple of years dating we were married. We bought a house in her hometown where she worked nearby.

I inherited a thirty-five mile commute to my job. Two years later, we had a daughter on the way.

I'll never forget that moment when my daughter entered this world. After nearly twenty-four hours of labor, a merciful doctor decided on a much-needed C-Section. I was in attendance for the whole procedure. The incision of the abdomen, the pinning back of the opening, the blood, the afterbirth, and then a purple little being that could have easily been from another planet popping into existence. A few cries later saw this purple alien take on a pinkish hue. She now had a look more like her mother and father than a space traveler from Mars. I was the father of a baby girl!

The first major change in my life was being a father! Suddenly the most important thing in life isn't yourself or your needs, it's the needs of another, and that "other" needs all the help possible. The responsibilities of fatherhood are challenging but definitely rewarding. My daughter grew up being loved by her mother, father, and her grandparents. We took a trip to Florida where my daughter Chelsea learned to take her first few strokes in a swimming pool. We'd take turns holding her in the pool, coaxing her to swim to each other. It was only a few strokes, but the competitive nature sprung forth as she tried to make it from mother to father and vice versa. When Chelsea was eighteen months old, I played a game of "Hide n Seek" around some parked cars at a tennis tournament with her. I was still young at heart and loved playing games with her. Little did I know, it would be the last time we would ever play this game.

I was thirty-two years old and it may seem strange to some, but was in the best shape of my life. I was also playing some of the best tennis of my life. I had been playing doubles with my wife's brother, Simon. Simon was two years older and we had become a good team. He had been a very good college tennis player.

We played in a money tournament in a town in Iowa called Dubuque. We played all day and had advanced to the semifinals. The sun was starting to set and we had to play one more match. We were playing two brothers, each of whom played in the top spot on their college teams. The winner of this match would be in the finals. One of the players had played number one for USC and was named Pac Ten player of the Year. He had just graduated a few months earlier.

When he was younger, he had at one time been the number one ranked junior player in the U.S.

We played our match at a country club on a beautiful court that was built in a pit. There were brick walls on all four sides, and all the spectators were above you looking down. The club itself sat just above this court. It was no accident that we were assigned this court. People from throughout the town came out that evening to watch the highly successful USC player and his brother demolish Simon and me. The weather was perfect. Fans surrounded the court. There were over a hundred people watching (of which perhaps three were rooting for us). It was a match I will never forget. Every point was well played. The games were close and the sets were close. We had chances to win both sets, but in the end we succumbed 7-5, 7-6. In the process, I think we won over many of the fans. They applauded a good point even if it happened to be won by us.

Funny the way things sometimes work out in life. This was the most memorable match I had ever played. This was one of the best matches I had ever played. Had our opponents been off at all, we would have won. I played tennis because it was fun. Even in that loss I was happy. I would have loved to win, but playing well and losing never made me lose any sleep.

Four days after that match, on a Wednesday, I finished up my last day of work at UPS. I was preparing to take my wife and daughter for two weeks of sun and fun in Corpus Christi the following day. I had worked the night shift at UPS and afterward went out with some co-workers for lunch and a few drinks.

I remember how incredibly tired I was on the way home. I hadn't slept much the night before, and the beers had only made things worse. I was most of the way home when I began to feel the car rumble. My eyes flew open to see my car leaving the road at 60 MPH and heading for the ditch. I only had a fleeting moment, less than a second, not enough time to do anything but prepare for the next moment. There was an embankment and no time to avoid it or slow down before impact. It was so surreal. The emotion of fear was non-existent. A more primitive reaction filled my being that emotion was simple and uncomplicated. It was mere survival. Perhaps it's the same thoughts an animal goes through when running from a predator.

Fear is an emotion that the brain needs time to process. Survival is the dominant emotion in our soul. Fear is only practical in avoiding situations that put one's life at risk. Once one's life is at risk fear only hinders the ability to survive. The prey that feels fear may freeze and involuntarily allow the predator to pounce. I felt no fear at this moment. As the car became airborne, all my mind was thinking was to become one with the car; to roll as it rolled, not to fight a battle that I had no way of winning. My chest restraint kept me in the car, but I hadn't clicked on my lap belt, and that left me bouncing from ceiling to seat. In a tight fetal position, I bounced and rolled. When the car finally stopped, I found myself no worse for the wear.
The car was destroyed. The driver's area had been crushed around me so tight that my head lay pinned on the dash by the car's roof.

The thought of how easily my head could have been popped like a melon had the roof caved just a smidgen more. This thought would send shivers through my body for months to come. I lay there unable to move, my head locked awkwardly on the dash. I now had time. Time to evaluate my situation and time to ponder what could have happened. I tried to unlock my head from the dash but to no avail. I tried to move but something made this impossible. I could see a small amount of blood on my knee, but felt no pain. I felt no pain at all. Amazingly, I had taken my car at 60MPH off an embankment, had rolled it numerous times down a deep ditch, smashed the car into the shape of a crushed tin can, and somehow not only survived, but also found myself unscathed by the whole ordeal. "What a miracle!" I thought. All the surrealism I once felt was now being replaced with reality.

I could hear voices. They called to me, "Are you OK? Are you OK?" I replied "Yes", and strained to turn my head, but it was fixed. I could only listen as a female's voice told me they had called 911.

It would be forty five minutes before the ambulance could get to me. I had time to reflect on my situation. I went from body part to body part evaluating my present condition, and found it odd that I couldn't seem to move my legs or my arms. "They must be trapped," I thought. "Surely they aren't damaged or I would feel the pain!"

I strained my eyes as best I could trying to see my body. From the corner of my eye I could just barely see my legs, but they didn't seem trapped at all. There was a small amount of blood on my knee, but my legs looked fine. I again tried to move them, but nothing. I couldn't feel them either. I stared at my legs as if they weren't even mine, but who else's legs could they be? They had to be mine.

A thought came to mind. "Is it possible that I am paralyzed?" I immediately thought back to that movie I saw in College and just as quickly dismissed it from my mind. "I'm not paralyzed! Something like that could never happen to me! There must be another explanation!"

It seemed an eternity. Unable to move my head or body, I was consoled by the voices that called 911. They told me not to move and that an ambulance would be there soon. I could hear the vehicles as they pulled up. Suddenly there were voices all around me, each one telling me to remain still.

I could hear them as they walked around the car. I heard them call for the "Jaws of Life." Suddenly the noise around me became deafening. It sounded as if I had just entered a construction zone as the saw from the Jaws of Life worked about. The vibration was shaking my skull as it lay pressed tightly against the roof and dash. Once again I heard voices tell me, "Don't move!" Then the pressure from the roof lifted. My head was finally free! I hadn't moved my head for nearly an hour. I couldn't resist the temptation to lift it now. I could see uniformed men all around me.

Moments later my head was stabilized by Paramedics; I was being prepared to be lifted onto a stretcher. I think back on that moment, often wondering if lifting my head played any part in the severity of my eventual outcome. I'd like to think it didn't, but it's a question that will never be answered. I was on my back in the rear of the ambulance when a young man began asking me questions. I always prided myself on my ability to control my mind and to remain relaxed, even in tough situations. This was a quality I learned from playing sports, and I was sure it was helping me remain calm now. I answered each question posed, but couldn't seem to keep my jaw from shaking. I remember the Paramedic telling me I was in shock. I saw the needle go into my arm and moments later felt the world around me become hazy. My eyes slowly closed.

I lifted my eyelids to find bright lights all around me. I gazed above me the best I could. There were dark outlines of faces standing all around me. I don't know if it was due to the drugs I'd been given, but everyone was in a shadowy outline with no details at all. It felt as though I was living a dream, or perhaps, a nightmare. It felt like one of those stories a person might tell when claiming to be abducted by aliens. The brightness of the lights made me squint.

I was amazed at the number of people that were surrounding my bed. They appeared to be Doctors and Nurses. My head was still hazy, perhaps from the accident or the drugs that were coursing through my veins. I lay on my back, dumbfounded at all the attention. The dark figures were talking amongst themselves, but for some reason I couldn't yet understand what they were saying. They continued to speak, seemingly unaware that I had now re-gained consciousness. Again, a weird, surreal feeling came over me. It seemed like a bad dream, but deep in my soul I knew it wasn't. I wasn't ready to accept the fact that I had put myself in such a terrible position. I still held fast to the belief that somehow I would get out of this. I couldn't possibly be par-alyzed, because from what I learned from that movie, there is no overcoming a spinal cord injury. Surely I wasn't meant to spend my life as a Paraplegic or perhaps even a Quadriplegic.

I heard a voice, a soft voice, tell me "you were in a car accident." The same voice continued saying "You have broken your neck in three places. The Cervical bones 5, 6, and 7. We believe there has been some damage to your Spinal Cord."

You would think that I would be crushed by this devastating news, but I remember a sense of acknowledgement. Although in denial, I already suspected my spinal cord was injured and now with this confirmation I could begin to accept it and begin my quest to overcome this difficult hand I'd been dealt. The rest of this day and the next were all like a dream. The chemicals siphoning through these plastic tubes and into my blood kept me tired and unable to fully comprehend my situation. These days were a series of recollections rather than a continuous sequence of events.

The Doctor said that an MRI needed to be done to know the severity of my Spinal Cord damage. Once completed, he would be better able to assess what needed to be done to improve my situation. I was about to go on an eerie adventure. Still not feeling completely aware of my surroundings, I found myself being rolled into a tight cylindrical tube. An eternity seemed to have passed before I was eventually taken back out. I remember the doctor talking to me from a speaker as the pinging of the machine rang in my ears. I remember later a friend telling me how difficult it would have been for him to be in such a tight space for 45 minutes, but to be totally honest it really wasn't a big deal. There were many more pressing issues in my life at the time other than claustrophobia.

I had been admitted to the Intensive Care Unit, commonly referred to as the ICU. It had only been a short time since I was taken out of the MRI to my bed. I assumed the drugs were cut back because my head seemed to be clearing, and things seemed much less like a dream and more like the world I was accustomed to.

The doctors wanted to have a conversation with me and felt it important that I have my wits about me. My wife Cindy was at my bedside as the doctor told me that an operation was needed to fix the damage done to my spine. Since the injury was in the neck my condition was considered Quadriplegia. He continued explaining that he planned to remove the imbedded bone then take bone from my left hip and use that bone to replace the three damaged vertebrae. He would also be fusing the damaged vertebrae to stabilize the area.

I'm not sure how I remember that last part. It seemed I couldn't get past the word he mentioned just before it, Quadriplegia. A person suffering from Quadriplegia is considered a Quadriplegic. My mind was going a thousand miles an hour. I had been in denial. I truly believed there was going to be some type of escape possible, but according to the doctors there wasn't. Future scenarios of my life raced through my head. Questions like: "Will I ever walk again?" "Will I be able to hug and play with my daughter?" "Will I ever have sex again?" and perhaps worst of all "Will people accept me as normal ever again?" I worked each summer teaching tennis to children. Will I be able to continue? If I do, how will the kids accept me and how effective can I be?

I'll never forget the words the doctor said as he continued speaking. "During the operation I will be entering through the front of your neck and will need to pin back your vocal cords. There is a chance that these cords could become damaged. There is a possibility that you may never speak again." I lay there, completely immobile, not a twitch of a toe, unable to change my position in bed. Now he's telling me I need an operation that may also take away my ability to speak. I pondered the implications of this worst-case scenario, unable to move, unable to speak and thereby unable to fully communicate. What a horrid existence that would be. What seemed to me like minutes or hours passed, but in reality it had only been a few seconds. I replied, "Yes, I would like the surgery," and my wife signed the papers. I was still in survival mode and I still believed I needed to do whatever it took to beat this. My surgery was scheduled for later that day.

It was in the evening of that first day that I got prepped for surgery. My doctor felt the sooner the operation, the better the potential outcome. My parents, brothers, sisters, and my wife were in attendance. The doctor entered the room with a few words before heading into surgery. He said that my seventh vertebrae had exploded into my Spinal Cord and it was his hope that by removing the fragmented bone lodged therein that my hands might improve. I remember how desperately I wanted my hands back. I tried moving my fingers or closing my hands but they just laid there, motionless.

Only a day ago I could run, walk, and move each finger independently. It is so strange to concentrate with all your might to move just a simple finger and see nothing happen. I could move my wrist a little bit, but my hands were lying there lifeless. I wanted this surgery and I wanted my hands back. I didn't even give the possibility of being mute a second thought. I could never let myself believe that that was my fate. I gazed around the room to see my sisters and mother all teary eyed, but I was fine. I was motivated and looking forward to waking up later, perhaps getting my hands back.

The anesthesiologist administered the sleeping potion and within moments my world once again became hazy and then totally black. I was carted into the operating room.

I opened my eyes. It seemed like just moments after being put out, but it had actually been hours. I was feeling much like I did when I awoke in the hospital. I was a bit disoriented and not sure exactly where I was. It slowly came back to me: the accident, the operation, being paralyzed. Moments later the doctor entered my room "Everything went well" he said. I tried to speak, but my voice was hoarse. I tried to talk but all I could muster was a very, very, soft whisper. My doctor felt my voice would get stronger over time, but there were no guarantees.

I think doctors would rather deny patients any hope so that they are happy with whatever improvement they get. I tried my hands. Perhaps my hands were all better and perhaps the rest of my body would soon follow. I tried with all my might to make my hands work the way they used to. There was no apparent change in my hands. I convinced myself that it was just going to take time.

The next few days would be a battle for my health. When I watched that film "Other Side of the Mountain" I don't remember them explaining all the side effects of altering your entire nervous system and going from being very active to non active. My first problem was that I was running a fever of 102 to 104 degrees. A specialist worked with me to keep my temperature under control. Dr. Wild would visit me many times each day very concerned about my elevated temperature. I was being given heavy doses of a steroid called Prednisone. Prednisone is a heavy-duty steroid that does a great job at reducing swelling.

The bones in your spinal column are designed to encapsulate and fully protect the spinal cord much the same way the cranium protects the brain. The problem with fully enclosing the spinal cord is that if any injury does occur and there's swelling, there's no place for the swelling to go. It becomes trapped within the bone. The pressure creates massive amounts of injury to the spinal cord just as it can to the brain. If you can minimize swelling to the spinal cord or the brain, a better recovery can usually be expected.

Prednisone was Dr. Wild's number one suspect for my fever, but still he searched everything. He was always doing tests on me and it seemed I was giving blood constantly. I also had a Respiratory Therapist. She was a girl in her twenties who would show up three times a day, usually wearing tight spandex and as fit as you could imagine. She was a beautiful girl and her name was Gina. She was passionate about her work much the same way Dr. Wild was. Gina would bring me a large tube inhaler with fumes that I would take deep into my lungs. This sounds easy, but it was far from it. My diaphragm was paralyzed and it caused my breathing to be short and shallow. She would hold the apparatus as I sucked in every last fume possible. She also gave me a lung capacity test called an Incentive Spirometer. This was also a large tube with a ball inside. You try to blow as hard and as long as you possibly can. Along the side are measurements much like a measuring cup. You keep the ball elevated as high and for as long as you can. This became an obsession for me. I was miserably poor in the beginning, but made slight improvements over the next few days.

Gina explained in detail just how important these treatments were. People in my condition, Quadriplegia, were likely to develop breathing problems that could become pneumonia. This could be life threatening and would significantly slow down my body's ability to begin healing. This was my first opportunity to begin working towards my recovery. I gave every treatment my best. I couldn't help but think that being in great condition at the time of my accident gave me a leg up on my treatments. I think if you were to ask Gina or Mr. Wild, they would say I was a very good patient.

CHAPTER TWO
The Realization

It had only been a little over twenty-four hours since my accident. I was in the ICU. I was taking breathing treatments over the course of the day. I had Dr. Wild working to keep my temperature under control, and I had the most amazing nurses a person could ever imagine. The fever kept me thirsty throughout the day. Since I couldn't hold a glass or can, the nurses would hold my drink and slide the straw into my mouth. I had trouble in the beginning. I had to re-teach myself how to suck through a straw. I had two basic problems. My first problem was just getting anything to come out of the straw. My second and more pressing problem was that once I did manage to suck some liquid into my mouth, I had trouble swallowing it. I hacked and coughed many times as my throat fumbled its way through the swallowing process.

I was so thirsty all the time and felt so guilty taking so much time from the nurses who had to stand there until I was finished. So on the third day I came up with an idea. I talked to my main nurse and explained to her my fabulous idea. She grabbed three new straws and through some finagling inserted one straw into another until an eighteen inch long straw was created. She then put the can of Cranberry juice on my bedside table and inserted one end in the drink and the other into my mouth. She stayed and watched to see if our wondrous creation would work. I sucked and sucked and sucked. I could see the red liquid as it was rising to the arch in the straw, but just couldn't seem to find its way over. My paralyzed diaphragm just didn't allow me the strength to carry the liquid to my awaiting mouth.

We simultaneously had the solution to our problem. Obviously, the table was too low and required far too much sucking power from me. She pulled the latch and raised the table up until it was higher than my head, and we tried again. I lay there on my back and once again sucked with all my might. Funny how sometimes when you fix one problem, you create a much different and larger one. The red cranberry juice flew over the arch and into my throat, so quickly and with so much force that I was overwhelmed. My injury had severely limited my ability to swallow and now my mouth was filled with juice and I just couldn't swallow fast enough. To make matters worse, when I stopped sucking, the juice didn't stop flowing. It kept flowing into my mouth without slowing down a bit. I inadvertently created the same situation used to siphon a gas tank. I was actually terrified. For a matter of seconds I felt I was going to drown. I've heard stories of how the Government took terrorists and had them water boarded. Water boarding is basically running water over a person's face simulating the effect of drowning. I can totally understand why it is such an effective way of extorting information and why there was some concern that it's a torture too extreme to be justified.

My nurse and I had just unintentionally designed and implemented a crude form of water boarding, and I was the one being tortured. I was terrified that I was going to drown in a sea of red cranberry juice. I couldn't get the straw out of my mouth, and my torture lasted about five seconds before the nurse came to the rescue. I know this story may sound funny, but until you are in a situation where you can't breathe, you don't truly understand what a terrifying feeling it is. I don't think I scare easily, but the helplessness I felt during those brief seconds scared me to death. It brought to light a sense of vulnerability I hadn't felt before. From that day on the nurses would just have to bear with me as I begged for liquids all day every day.

It had only been forty-eight hours since I first opened my eyes in ICU. The Intensive Care Unit limited the number of people who could visit me to just family and extended family. My brothers and sisters were visibly shaken up when they dropped in to see me, but what happened later that night really brought the severity of my situation to light. My mom was a wreck, but my mom was a very emotional loving human being who could cry at a drop of a hat. I expected her to cry. It made me sad to see her so devastated and know it was because of me. Her hands shook as she talked to me.

I didn't know it at the time, but my mom and dad had already talked to the doctor. They were told that I would never walk again. He said to them, "It's more likely that he will walk into a convenience store and buy a winning lottery ticket than it is he will ever walk again." I, at the time, had much higher hopes than that.

A realization of my condition happened that night. It came when my brother-in-law Simon and sister-in-law Brenda came for a visit. I talked to Simon as Brenda watched, and then I began talking to Brenda. These were two people I knew very well. We traveled on weekends to tennis tournaments together. Simon was my doubles partner and Brenda was a friend and one of my wife's best friends. After speaking with Simon my eyes looked toward Brenda. Her face was red and her eyes were swollen. I looked into her eyes as she began to speak. She muttered just a few words of her sentence when she fell apart. She began bawling, turned and walked out of the room (or should I say, scampered out). My heart was empty. Like a lead ball crashing into my head, the realization of a life of dependency hit me and hit me hard.

Brenda was a very levelheaded person whose opinion I valued greatly. When I saw her leave the room in tears I knew I was in trouble. I felt a tinge of doubt overcome me. It was a good thing in retrospect. The only way to fix a problem is to acknowledge one exists. I hadn't acknowledged just how severe my injury was. I was in denial, somehow thinking that if I didn't believe it happened then maybe it didn't. The fact was, it did, and this helped bring it to heart.

It was getting late and the visiting hours had long passed. I still had painkillers running through me. I was hooked up to a machine that gave a jolt of Morphine at the touch of a button. I couldn't push the button myself, but the nurses were more than happy to indulge me. There were limitations to how often I could receive this, however. I had no pain, no pain whatsoever, but I still took my quota of Morphine. I never took it for the pain; I took it for its' ability to take me to a place other than reality. I didn't like reality. I wanted to forget this ever happened. I'd rather sleep than be awake. When I was asleep I was free. When I was awake I was a prisoner to a seemingly lifeless body within a jail called a bed. Perhaps I'd eventually awake to find myself at home and uninjured. Maybe I'll get up and go jogging tomorrow. Maybe!

I was awakened to see a friend named David and his son Deepak. Deepak played tennis on the High School tennis team. My eyes were groggy and their voices sounded almost foreign. I was so tired. I wanted them to know I was grateful for their visit, but I wanted to sleep so badly. They had heard of my accident and snuck into the ICU to see me. I think I passed out on them, but I truly appreciated their visit. I had taught Deepak tennis since he was a little kid. It was one of many magnificent gestures that kept me strong and positive in my long journey ahead.

The next day my friend Randy was standing next to my bed. He had flown in from Dallas where he worked as a Chemical Engineer. We had been friends growing up. We became friends through basketball and tennis. I could see in his face he was fighting back tears. We both shared a passion for sports. He would later tell me that when word got to him about my accident, he realized that it could just as easily have been him. Life is continually teaching us lessons and when it seems there are no lessons to be learned, it is perhaps teaching lessons to those around us.

That night, like every night, was filled with being wakened, repositioned, and then falling back to sleep. This happened every two hours for the rest of the evening. This was a typical night for the next month or two. This prevented bedsores, which can lead to more serious conditions. Bedsores are hard to heal and easily infected. My caretakers were excellent and I never developed skin problems. I would see many others that weren't so fortunate.

I opened my eyes to the sun's rays fighting through the shades of my hospital room window. It was early, but it was evident that the nurses had already been quite busy in my room.

When I had the surgery on my neck that first day, a Halo was installed. A Halo is an apparatus that stabilizes the neck to prevent any further damage. Surrounding my forehead was a metal ring held tight to my skull by four large screws. The screws went through my skin and directly in the bone of my cranium. This was connected directly to a hard, fur-lined vest about my chest. It is called a Halo. A Halo would limit even an able bodied person from moving freely, it had little effect on me, I wasn't going anywhere anyway.

Pushing my eyeballs from one corner of my eye to the next, I surveyed my room. I could just make out some flowers next to the sunlit window. Moments later my nurse came through the door pushing a large cart. She said she was going to raise the head of the bed slightly. She reached to the side and I could hear the hum of the electric bed as my head slowly began to rise. My mind started swimming and my eyes began to blur. The humming ceased and I fought the dizziness that was trying to overcome me. My nurse explained that the goal was to eventually get me into a wheelchair, but that it would be a process of steps. My body had been lying down for the past few days. Damage to the spinal cord meant capillaries that help push blood through my body no longer worked properly. This caused my blood pressure to take a nosedive. Raising my head too quickly in this condition wouldn't allow enough pressure to push blood to my brain and would result in me blacking out. The dizziness I felt was the beginning stages of this. Over the course of the next few hours my head was raised in small increments allowing my body to adjust. Eventually I was sitting up in my bed and it felt amazing. So many things I've taken for granted in my life. The ability to just sit up was one. I looked at my entire room for the first time.

This was about the sixth day since my arrival at the hospital. This was my first time to sit up and see where I was. I had been taken out of the ICU and transferred to another room. There were two chairs, my bed, a television, a shelving unit, and a glorious window cascading sun beams against the wall. I gazed around the room in disbelief. There were flowers everywhere. Potted flowers of every color were all arranged in every corner and along every wall. I sat there and counted twenty-seven potted plants all attached with cards addressed to me. I had been isolated in my little world in the ICU, completely unaware that life went on outside these walls. People had heard of my car accident and had sent all this to me. I was never one to cry easily, but a tear rolled down my cheek followed by another right behind it. I never could have imagined that this many people would have cared enough or taken the time to make this incredible gesture of support. This was another step toward my recovery, and when I say recovery I don't mean to walk. I mean to find acceptance of my situation. It's easy to confuse acceptance with giving up. I had no plans on giving up, but my mind needed to find peace. Acceptance does not mean confining yourself to a certain outcome.

There is enormous healing power in the realization that you are loved. I felt that power, and this was yet another step towards building up my inner strength to fight this battle. Accepting your situation is necessary if you plan to fight, because without it you don't have a full understanding of what exactly it is you're fighting.

My breakfast was brought in and set down on the same type of table that tried to drown me a number of days earlier. I was still battling a fever and my appetite was non-existent. I picked through a few things with the encouragement of my nurse, but left the majority for the garbage. Food didn't taste right. Food actually had no taste at all. It was like eating cardboard. The doctors were never able to explain why my taste buds went on a two-month hiatus, but even my favorite foods lost their luster. In the coming weeks my brothers and sisters would bring me Harris Pizza, the best pizza in the world, but it wouldn't taste the same. My injury somehow affected my ability to taste. The nurse helped me pick out my meals for the week. I chose to eat primarily fruits and juices.

The next couple of days were a combination of Doctor Wild visiting my room determined to rid me of this mysterious fever and my Respiratory Therapist shoving tubes in my mouth and telling me to inhale. Each passing day I found my lungs to be just a bit stronger. A Physical Therapist was also added. She came with stretch bands in an attempt to strengthen my arms. My arms could move but were very weak. My biceps were weak, but my triceps were nearly non-existent. She would hold one end and wrap the other around my wrist. I would pull with all I had, but it was clear I had a long road ahead of me.

On the seventh day, not long after I had picked through another afternoon lunch, a couple of nurses arrived at my door. It was time to sit in a wheelchair. They brought with them a small plank-like board, which I would come to know as a "Sliding Board". The sliding board acts like a bridge, linking the surface where a person is to the place a person wants to be. In my case, the sliding board was wedged below my butt and the wheelchair. They tied a gait belt around my waist and then working in unison, and keeping me balanced, they slid me in a sitting position onto the wheelchair. Once in the wheelchair they wrapped a tight belt around me connecting me to the chair and keeping me from falling out.

It was important for me to sit up a portion of each day to maintain good blood pressure. This lowered the possibility of me blacking out.

I had learned to hate the bed I was in. It was my prison. I could have just as easily been handcuffed to a wall in a dungeon. I had been lying in bed for multiple days, unable to turn, unable to move. Sitting up was nice, but I wanted more. What a feeling to escape from that prison they called a bed. My nearly lifeless arms weren't strong enough to push the chair on my own, but it was great just sitting up in it.

The next day, after my noontime lunch, my nurse Sandy walked in the door carrying a pile of letters. She told me these letters were being held until now, and she was going to read them to me. What a beautiful soul Sandy was to sit and read all these letters to me. There were nearly thirty letters and she read every one. Letter after letter wished me well. These were from students I had coached, fellow teachers, parents and friends. I was like a dried up sponge and these letters were inspirational water that I was soaking into my soul. I think sometimes it takes everything to be taken away from youbefore you can truly appreciate all the things that are given. Each letter touched my soul like no letter before ever had. Towards the end of the stack, the nurse began reading this particular letter. I will paraphrase it because I no longer have it, but it went something like this:

"Mr. Moore, I wanted to thank you for all you've done for me. When I was in high school I was drinking and doing drugs and really had no plans for the future. I joined the tennis team and you cared about me. When I was missing practice you were strict and forced me to make a decision between committing to the team or otherwise being taken off the team. I chose to be on the team. You made an impression on me and now I have finished college and have a good job. I don't think this would have happened without you."

My eyes swelled up. The moisture caused my vision to blur. Emotion enveloped me, and I could feel the teardrops as they slowly formed and rolled down my cheek. This letter truly touched me in a way no other letter could. This was so unexpected. He was the last person I expected to receive a letter from. I remembered this young man vividly. I liked him a lot, but I was convinced that he hated me. He was the one that was always late for practice.

He was the one that almost missed an important meet because he stopped at a convenience store on the way to the bus. He made me work far more than I wanted to as far as discipline goes. I eventually told him to either get his act together or I would remove him from the team. I honestly expected him to take the latter, but to my surprise he was on time and present for every meet and practice from that day forward. I was stunned!

This simple letter opened my eyes to one of the most important things every person should know. You see, I went about my life doing the best I could. When I would play I would try my best, and when I coached I did the same. The culmination of receiving all those flowers, then all of those letters, and finally the gratitude from this young man of whom I was sure hated me, enlightened me to something I hadn't been aware of. We all go through life each and every day affecting other peoples' lives. We can be a positive influence and/or a negative one. Each interaction with others can have huge effects. I'm sure there were plenty of times I had negative impacts on others, but I was now finding out all of the positive influences I had as well. Most of us take it for granted, but each day we make a bigger difference than we could ever imagine. Every impact we have with another person can be magnified as that person goes through their life. This made me want to be a more positive influence. I wanted to make a good impact on others. I may not be perfect, but from that point on I was a better person than I was before. I hope I never forget the feeling of empowerment I felt that day. I remind myself of this day often.

One afternoon, my wife came to visit me with one of her teacher friends. I was lying on my back, looking through the vertical bars that made up my Halo. I was looking forward to the visit. Talking to people was a good way of keeping my mind off all these other problems. My head was locked due to the Halo and I could only see people when they leaned over my bed unless of course the head of the bed was up. I had a permanent view of the hospital ceiling when lying down. Thus, most of their visit was completely verbal for me. They stayed for maybe a half an hour to an hour. During that time my wife's friend complained about all her problems, which amounted to nothing.

She went on and on about all these trivial things that seemed to be bothering her. I remember it vividly. I was just thinking how ridiculous all her complaints were. She complained about the most trivial of things, so trivial I can't remember one that I could mention as an example. It seemed to me she had lost her way when it comes to life. There are so many things to be grateful for and that should be where her mind was, not dwelling on all those things she'd rather have changed. It crossed my mind that she should look at my situation and realize just how trivial her problems were. Perhaps she would see what a wonderful life she actually had, but she could only see her own situation. Empathy is an important thing to attain in life. It allows you to reach out to others. Without it you will only dwell on yourself. During the next five months I would find myself surrounded by patients much worse than myself and I would find that my ability to empathize with others had grown much stronger due to my accident. It would keep my mind humble. It would help me appreciate the things I had, and not dwell on the things I didn't. Gratitude is one of the most powerful qualities a person can have. Always be thankful, always!

In a few days I was moved to Genesis West, part of the Genesis hospital system. Genesis West had a Rehabilitation floor. Until then, a typical day was eating my fruits and juices, being repositioned every couple hours by the nursing staff, taking medications, giving blood ,and of course, the nightly routine. Before I had ever been injured I probably moved my bowels twice a week, but the hospital staff was dead set on me moving my bowels every night. They would give me Senokot to help push this process along. I would take stool softeners. I would be given special liquids, all in an attempt to get things going.

When it was time for me to sleep one nurse would balance me on my side while the other nurse wedged pillows behind my back so that I would remain balanced on my side. They then placed an incontinence bed pad behind me, tucking it up under my lower hip and laying it out across the bed. Later in the night, once the medications took effect, a thick liquid would be expelled from my body and the nurses would clean me up and throw away the bed pad, replacing it with a clean one.

I could never feel any of this happen. I assumed it was just the way things were going to be. This was a degrading thing for me. I felt I had lost my independence and my dignity. I felt bad about myself every night after this "nightly routine". This was the hardest thing for my morale. I tried to not let it get me down, but it was difficult. I think most of us feel pride on being independent, regardless of what it is.

As the week progressed, Dr. Wild and the Respiratory Therapist gave me a clean bill of health. It was time to leave my current hospital and move to the new one. I would now have a lot less machines in my room and it would feel more like home. It was now time to get to work and see what improvements I could make on this somewhat listless and stagnant body, passive would now be replaced by intensive exercise.

CHAPTER THREE
Rehabilitation

I was delivered via ambulance to my new hospital room and my family brought along my flowers to decorate the new room. I now had a TV with my own remote control that I would soon learn to place strategically by my side. I was still unable to see anything but the ceiling, the TV, and the upper levels of the walls in front of me. My new room had a nice big chalkboard with my schedule on it. Along with my schedule was the name of my Primary Nurse as well as my Physical and Occupational Therapists. My nurse, Judy, was small in stature, perhaps five foot four and had the build of a gymnast. She was fit and stronger than you could ever believe. Many a time she would almost single handedly get me up and in my wheelchair. Most of the time she would have help, and even some of the stronger men who worked the floor seemed to struggle more than Judy.

Judy introduced me to "Range Of Motion". I had been getting Range Of Motion up to this point without really knowing what it was called, but it became more intense and more often from this point on. Range of Motion is comprised of basically stretching out every part of your body. Your Achilles, Thighs, Quads, Back, and on and on. A full Range Of Motion would last a good half hour to an hour, and I totally fell in love with it. It was so good to see all my body parts moving, even if it took another person to move them. My Primary nurse Judy, along with Patty my PT and Chrissie my OT, all took turns giving me a good stretch every day. One common stretch done by all the therapists went like this. While lying on my back, the therapist would hold one of my knees down with her own knee.

She would press down on the opposite knee with her hand effectively locking it out. She could then cup my heel with her free hand and lean forward stretching my achilles tendon with her forearm. In this position she could then elevate this same leg over her shoulder and stretch my hamstrings. This would be repeated on the other leg. Stretches would be held to a count of fifteen and one by one all the major muscles groups would get a great stretch. It only took a few weeks for me to become more limber than I had ever been in my life.

When your muscles are paralyzed and completely flaccid there's little resistance to stretching. I was amazed to see how far the hospital staff could stretch my body. Stretching is necessary to keep blood flow moving into the muscles. It's also needed to allow a person to someday dress him or herself. One of the most important stretches is long sitting. You are sitting up with your legs straight ahead and locked, the therapist bends your upper body forward towards your feet. It's much like a parallel version of standing and touching your toes. I'm indebted to these stretches each time I put on my shoes and tie them. I gained so much from Range of Motion. I understand that some rehabilitation places don't focus on it as much as they should. It's my belief that Range of Motion is like priming a motor with gasoline. It stimulates the body, the blood flow, and works the muscles. In my opinion, if a person's body has the opportunity to regain movement, Range of Motion should play a big part in it.

Muscle spasms became more and more prevalent in my body as the days wore on. Spasms can be painful, but mine were not. Spasms are the body's way of keeping up the muscle tone in your body. The body is an amazing thing. I have learned to listen to my body. The body is always trying to repair itself. Let me say that again! The body is always trying to repair itself. It knew my muscles were wasting away and to combat this it began giving me spasms. Spasms tighten up the dying muscles in repetitious contractions much like a workout without the effort. There are some instances where the body may not be able to overcome the damage done to it, but it will try to make the most of it. I understand the people who took medication to quell spasms when they were painful, but in my mind I wanted these spasms. The spasms were keeping my muscles stronger than they would be otherwise.

The doctors were quick to prescribe muscle relaxers for me, but I refused. I would learn in the coming months how intense spasms can be. They can throw you out of your wheelchair. They can be stronger than even a regular controlled muscle contraction. Some may have thought me crazy, but I embraced spasms as a way of keeping my body strong and ready for my rehabilitation. I figured if I was going to regain my muscles, wouldn't it be nice if my muscles were already strong and ready to go even if my brain had no ability to control them?

As I mentioned earlier, my new room had a remote for my bed. The first morning in my new room I woke up and pressed the button to elevate the bed, thereby putting me in a sitting up position. I then pressed the TV remote and turned the TV on. Pressing any buttons on these remotes was quite a work out let alone pressing the right buttons. Once again, I couldn't see the remote while lying flat. My hands were badly impaired. Moving my arms took quite an effort, but I was proud when my many fumbling attempts resulted in my sitting up in front of the TV without the help of anyone.

The National news was on and they were covering a story from South Africa. A young white woman around twenty had been killed by a group of black people. The irony of the story was that she was in South Africa as part of a peaceful endeavor to denounce Apartheid and the racist actions Whites were committing against Blacks. She had finished her work and was now heading towards the airport to travel back to the States.

The story had me in tears. My thinking had changed drastically since my crash. I no longer felt a separation between my life and others. This woman's death could be felt in my heart as if it had happened to me. A series of events were set in motion that culminated in the death of this beautiful, loving woman. I could feel a connection, one that I never would have felt just weeks earlier. I questioned why the world is filled with so much pain and injustice. Is there a reason for everything that happens? Perhaps! I know plenty of people who would say there is, but still be unable to tell me exactly what that is.

I think you're fooling yourself if you think you understand exactly why things happen. I was beginning to look at my life and that of others differently. Like a veil removed from my eyes, I began seeing things much clearer.

Karma is an easy thing to believe when events happen to support it, but there are people who do bad things who often go unpunished. This woman died trying to fight for better treatment of all people.

You'll never convince me that life is fair, but did any good come from this girl's losing her life? Well, it touched me and made me a little better than I was even a few moments ago. Perhaps it touched others in the same way. Is there a reason? Maybe it's to teach a lesson to others. Life is a journey, a soulful journey. The only way to live it is striving to make oneself better. Her horrible death made me a little better person that day.

The reason why we should all make positive differences isn't for any earthly rewards, it's to do what you feel is right. To follow the path I believe is within all of us. To go against your path brings stress and uneasiness. I had lived with a lot of stress and uneasiness and now it was time to feel contentment. Perhaps it took breaking my neck to see this!

The hustle and bustle of the hallway signaled that morning had arrived. Soon my morning dish of fruit and cranberry juice was delivered. Judy arrived a little later, emptied my leg bag, moved me in the bed, washed her hands and helped feed me my breakfast. I could apply pressure to push a button on a remote, but picking up a grape or a piece of melon was not possible. My fingers were just straight and couldn't move independently so picking up anything was out of the question, and a spoon or fork was completely out of the question.

The first Rehab appointment in my life was at nine. Nurses came by about fifteen minutes early to get me into my wheelchair. The sliding board was kept in the corner of my room. A gait belt was wrapped around my waist. The sliding board was put into place and then with a "One", "Two", "Three" I slid across my wooden bridge landing safely in my wheelchair seat. Once again a gait belt tied me to the chair and I was pushed down the hallway to meet Patty, the woman who would be responsible for many breakthroughs in the coming weeks. Patty was short in stature and the darkest red hair you could imagine. Her face was kind and covered in red freckles. She was relatively new to Physical Therapy, and I found out that very first day she was a motivated go-getter that took her career much more seriously than just a job. She wanted to make a difference on that first day and each day afterward. She would push me. I loved it.

Most of the success I had in life came from self-motivation. I still had plenty of self-motivation, but now I had a teammate to keep me on track and help me reach my goals.

The first day was fifty minutes worth of trying to sit up on my own. It was a tricky thing. The feet have to be positioned apart just right and your weight has to be forward, leaning in over the legs with your elbows against the quads. She would situate me over and over again into a sitting position much like you'd do with a baby. I'm not sure what she was expecting, but I definitely didn't impress anyone. It was so weird to feel so unbalanced. My unhurt life was still fresh in my head, so sitting there wobbling all around until I finally fell to the mat was unsettling. I learned something very import- ant that day and it's still very important now. I learned how important it is to position your feet properly before undertaking any kind of movement. The nurses who had moved me into the wheelchair that very morning didn't understand. They used brute force to just lift me across the void and along the sliding board. I'm sure most all spinal cord patients figure out that there's an enormous amount of technique involved in accomplishing everyday tasks, and feet are at the top of the list.

My next appointment was with Chrissie. Chrissie was an Occupa- tional Therapist. I honestly had no idea what an Occupational Therapist was until I met her. Chrissie was a stark contrast to Patty. Patty was probably in her early thirties while Chrissie was in her early twenties. Chrissie had blonde hair that was shoulder length and curled under at the ends. She was an attractive girl, thin with a fair complexion. She was engaged and soon to be married. She was very professional and did a nice job, but lacked the passion that Patty had. Although I was very limited at the time, Chrissie worked with me on long sitting and touching my shoes. Patty and Chrissie both worked with me on strengthening my arms through elastic bands. My occupational and physical therapy overlapped quite a bit during these first meetings. Both therapists wanted to teach me to sit on my own, much like a toddler. They wanted to strengthen the parts that worked and inevitably this would come down to my arms. After a few days, Patty gave me a one-pound weight to work with while I was in my room. I would balance the handle in my palm and lift it up as many times with each hand as I could.

I dropped the weight many times on myself, but lucky for me it didn't hurt a bit. As a matter of fact, I didn't even feel it. I guess it was one of the advantages of being paralyzed.

It was five in the morning and the staff wouldn't be coming to my room for a while. I decided to try and watch some TV on my own. Doing even the simplest things like turning on the TV gave me a sense of accomplishment. I previously made an effort to remember where all the buttons and their functions were so I could operate it without needing to see it. As I mentioned earlier, pushing the buttons was especially difficult because my hands were paralyzed. I had trouble being able to feel the buttons and once I figured out what buttons were what came the challenge of pushing them. I would use my knuckles more than anything and press my hand into the remote, not much different than throwing a closed fist punch. Often I would inadvertently press numerous buttons, so repetition until I got it right was a necessity. The first step was to find the remote. I moved my hand along the bed until I finally felt the cord to the remote. This was the old fashioned type remote. I couldn't feel the remote itself but knew it was connected to the cord. I wedged the cord between my fingers and turned my hand slightly, then pulled, expecting the remote to come towards me, but it seemed stuck. I wasn't sure if it was caught on something. Perhaps I was lying on top of it. I pulled a little harder and it still wouldn't budge. I turned my hand a little more, further securing the cord in my hand and pulled with all my might, yet it didn't move an inch. I finally gave up and pressed the call button for a nurse. The call button was elevated so I could see that.

As my hand came up to hit the call button I saw a little blood on my fingers. It took a few minutes before the nurse walked through the door. I told her my remote to the TV was stuck and I couldn't dislodge it. She walked right over and picked up the remote from my side and showed it to me. It wasn't where I was trying to find it. She then looked down at my lower body and a look of disgust combined with horror cascaded across her face, confirming what I had already assumed. I hadn't been pulling on the cord to the remote. I had been pulling on the tube from my leg bag catheter.

These catheters are placed inside the penis and locked in with an inflatable balloon so they cannot be removed. I had spent the past 10 minutes pulling with all my might on the catheter tube locked inside my penis. I caused it to bleed. The sight of the blood on my hand and knowing where it came from made me sick to my stomach. It may not have hurt a bit, but I imagined how much it would have. I made a point to always have the television remote placed on the bedside table from that point on. Thank goodness my arms were so incredibly weak.

Judy came strolling in later that morning to write my new schedule on a chalkboard mounted across the room. My schedule reminded me of the schedules I received in Grade School. I had six (one hour) classes planned ahead of me, seven when you added in lunch. My day consisted of two hours of physical therapy, two of occupational therapy, and a couple of hours that changed periodically. My first class today was a card class. I was tired and weak, yet anxious to start my road to recovery. As I mentioned before, I have always believed in my abilities, at least since I've been an adult.

I had high hopes that I could somehow prove these so-called experts wrong, to find a way to overcome their dire predictions. Sometimes "Hope" overpowers logic. Sometimes hope is a way of dealing with very bad situations. No matter how bad the situation, the mind wants to believe there's a way to escape, to find an outlet that takes you to where you want to be. I wanted to be normal again. I wanted to sleep through the night. I wanted to go the bathroom myself without being drained by a tube or having my inner wastes turned to liquid so it could drain out onto a bed pad each night. I especially wanted to end getting my butt wiped and cleaned every night. I can't say whether I am typical or not, but I wanted to be in control of my life. Incontinence made me feel like a failure. I wanted my dignity back. My mind drifted back to that paralyzed skier in that movie. I thought it would be horrible and unimaginable suffering her situation, but I was only thinking of her inability to move her body. There are things far more debilitating than a lack of movement. I wanted my dignity, my self-esteem, and my life back. I just wanted to feel good about myself again.

CHAPTER FOUR
Stepping Out Onto That Road

I read a book called Maximum Performance when I was in high school. I read it to improve my ability to succeed in sports, but found it carried over nicely to everyday life. The book taught me that a focused mind was an important path towards being successful. It was written by a group of Olympic trainers and dealt with relaxation and mind control. No book has had a bigger impact on my life. It taught me to use breathing exercises to relax my muscles. It taught me how to control my mind by visualizing successful outcomes. I pride myself in my ability to control my thoughts and focus on the positive rather than the negative. I'm still surprised I went into shock after my accident. Maybe I still have some mental strengthening to do!

On my first full day of classes Judy began dressing me. Dressing is no easy task and takes more than one person. I was 200 pounds at the time of my injury, and now I weighed about 160 with most of that weight loss consisting of muscle. Dressing even a person of my weight, who can't shift their body or help in any way, is not easy. It is done with 2-3 people. One person is in charge of pulling the clothes on while the others rock the body back and forth. Through a series of pulling the clothes up, right-left, right-left, my pants get slid on. After my clothes are on it's time for yanking me across the sliding board to my wheelchair and off to my first class. Judy pushed me into a room the size of a typical classroom.

I was the last one to arrive and a couple of minutes late. The nurses would eventually get my routine down in the coming days and this would be the last time I was late for a class.

I was one of five patients, but the only Spinal Cord patient. In time, I found that the majority of patients I would be sharing therapy with were stroke victims. It's obvious that the other patients had partial paralysis like myself, but caused by a completely different injury. My problem comes from a functioning brain sending good messages to my body, only to have these messages unable to reach their destination because of a blockage of the signal (My damaged Spinal Cord). The Stroke patients have a damaged brain that is having trouble sending valid messages to the body, but whose connections are intact.

I was rolled up to a large round card table. Judy reached down and clicked on my brakes to my wheelchair. There were two men and two women already sitting at the table and they were in wheelchairs as well. The teacher of the class was about my age, in her early to mid thirties. Her long brown hair was straight and thick and stretched down to her lower back. She had a warm and caring face with a radiant smile. I got the impression that she truly enjoyed her job helping people. She began explaining that we were going to play a card game. I don't remember what the rules were and I'm not sure I remembered the rules while we were playing. The intent wasn't in the game anyway, but rather in the manipulation of the cards.

She dealt the cards out to each one of us and we all received a fairly large amount of cards, perhaps ten. The other four at the table were able to pick up their cards and place them in a wooden card holder that was on the table in front of us. I could tell their hands had trouble picking up the cards, but they were all successful and soon they had all their cards sitting nicely in front of them, some even arranged their cards. I made numerous attempts to pick up my cards, but each time I lowered my hands to the table the best I could do was nudge the cards along the surface with my knuckles.

The teacher took the time to help me get my cards up and in their holder. I really am understating the situation when I say she helped me, because in reality she pretty much did it herself. My hands were useless at picking up anything. Once my cards were sitting up in their holder, I was able to situate my hand so that I could slip the corner of the card between my fingers and place the card on the table. I say "place", but it was more like shaking my hand till the card fell from between my fingers.

This was far more difficult than it looked. I had to concentrate on so many things to get that card on the table. I had to think to move my arm. I had to think about my hand placement. Not that I could move my hand. I couldn't move my hand at all, but I could use my hand as an extension of my wrists.

The class frustrated me to no end. I enjoyed doing things fast and efficiently all my life and I just hadn't developed the patience for tedious tasks that take far longer than they should. I was easily the most limited person at the table, and again the realization of my situation pounded into my head. I had so far to go just to catch up with the people at my table. My best explanation is that I temporarily fell into a state of insanity. My life had changed in so many ways, but I had a lot of work to do when it came to patience. It's so hard to be unable to accomplish a task you've done throughout your life with relative ease. A loud voice inside me was screaming to avoid this situation. This exercise exposed my disability and re-enforced the painful reality of my situation, but my calmer voice kept telling me to keep working. Things will get better. Learn to be patient and give it some time.

I was excited for the hour to end. physical therapy was next, and anything that started with the word "physical" sounded good to me. Soon I was rolling on down to the end of the hall, which was also the dropping off point for occupational therapy as well.

I knew I would need to embrace all the different aspects of therapy, but this was what I looked forward to. I was ready to give it my all, and from the previous week, Patty already knew I was up for a good work out. Patty wheeled me to the elevated mat. It looked similar to the wrestling mat that was rolled up behind the house while growing up except it stood on four legs like a table. My brother was an avid wrestler and eight years older than me. I was probably about ten when he purchased a large wrestling mat and stored it in the backyard. He'd unroll it on occasion, and kids from around the neighborhood would come over to wrestle.

Derryl taught me to wrestle back then and had even taken me to a wrestling tournament. He enjoyed having me wrestle the neighbor kids, many of whom were much older than me. I don't remember losing very often, but perhaps that's just selective memory on my part. Now, in therapy, was a similar mat except this one looked much more like a bed.

Patty tied my gait belt around my waist. She then positioned my feet and slid me across the sliding board with an ease that would have made my other nurses envious. Positioning of the feet is the key. It was then, and still is. After some minor stretching, Patty placed me at the edge of the mat with my feet on the ground.

She began placing cones around my feet at varying distances. My goal was to try to touch the top of the cones without falling from a sitting position. Much like the previous week's therapy this is an awkward and unusual feeling. The stomach muscles that would normally give you stability are non-existent, so you must find ways to compensate. Something that all spinal cord patients learn is how to use their body, arms, elbows, and feet to make up for a lack of core.

The following weeks were dominated by this exercise. Sitting with legs draped over the edge of the mat, trying to touch the top of every cone. As one got touched, Patty placed it farther away. In a matter of weeks I was reaching cones far further than I ever imagined, and it came from placing my feet properly for stability, using my opposite elbow against my knee and sometimes placing my opposite hand against the mat.

Trying to find that balancing point that was taken for granted over the course of my life was hard. Taken for granted because my stomach and core muscles did all the work for me. I didn't realize just how important this fundamental exercise was, but I do now. Each time I dress or reach for something, these skills allow me to be independent. To gain a bit of the dignity associated with accomplishing a task on my own, we also worked on strengthening my arms and even pushing my own chair.

In therapy, the words Quadriplegic or Paraplegic are rarely used. We have nicknames and are known as a "Quad" or a "Para". Much simpler and everyone knows what we're talking about. I remember when Patty first rolled in my own special chair. It was a "Quad" chair. The push rims weren't smooth, but instead had knobs sticking out every few inches. These are also called "Projection Rims" and are made specifically for people like myself with little or no hand function. I got into the chair, put my hands in front of one of the knobs, and pushed. It was much easier than smooth rims.

The drawback on projection rims is that it's difficult to go fast and difficult to slow down when going downhill, but there really weren't any hills I needed to navigate, and I couldn't go much slower than I was already traveling.

My new projection rims allowed me to go places on my own. I could now go out in the hallway outside my room on my own. I loved just hanging out in the hallway watching all the people. I was desperately missing the freedom I was so accustomed to. I hated spending time in my room, especially the bed. As I mentioned before, it was a form of prison. I could go on and on about the upcoming weeks, but I will sum it up. I worked on strengthening, balance from a sitting position, and pushing my chair independently. My occupational therapy involved hand manipulation by handling small objects and exercises like putting nuts on bolts. Through my urging I was allowed to add a physical and an occupational class and eliminate the two "extra" classes. My daily tasks slowly improved with each passing day. After a month I could push my own chair to therapy and I was beginning to work on dressing myself.

My Occupational Therapist had straps affixed to the waistband of a couple of my sweat bottoms. Chrissie and Patty were working in tandem to teach me how to dress myself. My strength had improved greatly and I was even working on transferring myself without any help, but that was still a work in progress. The therapists had a new trick for me to work on. I would be lying on my back atop the mat with full Halo and vest, I would use my arms to rock the best I could from side to side. I looked much like the carp my father and I would catch out at the Hennepin canal.

My father always told me that when you catch a Carp you shouldn't return it to the water because they took food away from the fish we were trying to catch. I remember him throwing the Carp into the long grass and me watching it thrash back and forth for a while. Now I had become that Carp. I was just as helpless, thrashing back and forth on the mat. I could hear my Halo squeaking with every thrash and in time the bolts loosening. These loosened bolts were ground into my skull and were re-tightened occasionally.

Once a week a man from prosthetics would stop by while I was in therapy and tighten the four screws driven into my head. I dreaded those moments. He'd start turning his screwdriver. This was painful and created a strange and surprisingly loud sound, as the bolts would grind deeper and deeper into my skull. It resonated directly from the bone to my ear. You would think everyone in the Rehab room could hear this nails on a chalkboard sound, but it seemed no one ever did. It usually culminated with a droplet or two of blood rolling down my forehead.

To help with putting shoes and socks on I would work on "Long Sitting". I would lie on the mat with my feet extended over the edge and practice reaching towards my feet, thereby stretching out my hamstrings. Sitting with feet straight ahead and reaching my feet was no problem whatsoever.

To attempt dressing myself, I would start in long sitting position, draping my sweat pants around my feet. Then, with wrists locked onto the straps that were sewn to the sides of my pants, I would lay back and rock from side to side pulling as hard as I could. I couldn't help but laugh one day when a TV commercial had a girl using the same technique when trying to squeeze into some exceptionally tight jeans. I thought "Wow. I do it that way too!" I could sometimes get my pants to my knees, but never any farther. My rocking was pathetically inadequate to serve this purpose. I just wasn't strong enough, but even this limited success made me feel good.

This was good practice, but it never quite worked for me. I could reach my feet easily, but socks and shoes were too difficult to handle with my hands. I would continue to practice this routine on a daily basis. In the end, I needed to be dressed. I wasn't yet ready to dress myself.

Towards the end of the day when therapy was finished I would wander back to my room completely exhausted. I worked as hard as I could everyday. I found my accident not only took away feeling and strength, but my endurance as well. It took very little to get me out of breath. It reminded me of training to play basketball, tennis, or preparing to run the local Bix 7 road race. Had I worked this hard back then, I would have been much better at all these endeavors.

I was truly focused on my recovery. It wasn't just part of my life, like sports, it was my life! I knew whatever the future held for me, I wanted the best quality of life I could attain. I didn't know how much I could accomplish, but didn't want to have any regrets over how hard I worked. I had always tried to instill a similar work ethic in the kids I coached. You may not ever be good enough to be a professional, but you can always be better than you are right now. Although my hopes were of making a total recovery, I knew that my goal was to push myself as far as I could and see how much of my old life I could recover, whether that meant walking or just being able to dress on my own. I think it's important to realize what you can and can't control. I knew I had the power to improve, but how far that improvement would take me was partially out of my hands.

Returning from my last therapy of the day, the nurses would hurry and get me back into bed. It was their primary job to keep me healthy, and skin breakdown is always a major concern. I still hated being confined to my bed and increasingly stayed in my wheelchair to the chagrin of my nurses. Pressure sores from sitting long periods are a definite threat to people like myself. I was sitting on a Jay cushion that cost nearly four hundred dollars. It was heavy and made with gel to help alleviate pressure, but I still needed to get off my butt and lay on my side periodically. My therapies helped in this regard, because during the course of the day I was continually being taken out of my chair and put on the mat. This allowed oxygenated blood to flow across my buttocks to keep my skin cells alive and healthy. Sores develop when a portion of the body doesn't allow proper blood flow. Blood carries oxygen to the cells, and when the cells are starved for oxygen for too long they begin dying. Pressure sores are extremely difficult to heal because it's a portion of the body that has basically died and begins rotting away. Pressure sores that aren't caught in time can rot all the way to the bone and are susceptible to infection.

Many Spinal Cord patients die from complications involving the infection of pressure sores. Nurses were anxious to get me in bed at the end of the day, and I was anxious to stay in my wheelchair. A compromise was always struck, but I so hated those times lying on my side in bed unable to move. I had so much to accomplish. I just couldn't imagine this being my life in the years to come.

My nurses began allowing me to eat supper before going back to bed. It just seemed much more normal to eat sitting up rather than lying down, although an occasional breakfast in bed is never a bad thing, even before I got hurt.

After supper was the time my visitors would start dropping by. My family always made sure someone visited me each and every day. Most days numerous family members would come, but of course seeing my daughter was the highlight of the day. My Halo, which made me look akin to Frankenstein, scared my one and a half year old daughter to some extent. It made me sad to see her wary of me, but as time went by she became more and more accustomed to my new look.

Sleeping in the Halo was not an easy task. My head was suspended within the Halo and never touched the pillow, or anything for that matter. Once positioned in the bed I could not move. I was under constant sleep deprivation, but I still remember one strange side effect of the Halo. I'm not sure why I still remember it, but it was just so unusual. I would wake up each morning and my hair would be perfect. My hair never touched the bed or anything through the course of the day so once it was combed it stayed that way.

I received sponge baths occasionally. The Halo and vest were always left on so I wasn't able to take a regular bath or shower. My hair was almost never washed. One day two young girls who weren't actually nurses but more like nurse's aides came into my room. These girls were very young, early twenties if that. They both reminded me of college girls and when they came into my room they were all giddy. Both girls had straight black hair down to the middle of their back. They looked like they kept themselves active, sporting dark tans and seemingly very fit. They brought in numerous towels and filled basins from the faucet. It had been weeks since my hair had been washed and they were there to remedy that situation.

They decided to just leave me in my bed and used pillows to prop up my upper body. They laid bed pads across the mattress and put a small empty basin below my head. They laughed and giggled the whole time as one carefully poured cups of water on my head while the other tried to make sure the excess water went into the empty basin. I could tell from their "trial and error" technique that this was something they had never done before. The amount of plastic bed pads they had strewn across the bed made it virtually impossible that any water would reach my mattress. Once my hair was sufficiently wet they added the shampoo and each reached between the bars of my Halo and began massaging my scalp. I was in heaven. It felt so good to have my hair clean and even better to have my head massaged. This was definitely the highlight of my hospital stay to this point. The two girls finished by rinsing my hair the same way they had wet it to begin with. They then stayed and combed my hair into place.

At the end of each night, my visitors would leave and I was placed in bed. I would lie there facing the ceiling. I always started the night facing the ceiling. Lying on my back allowed me to use the one-pound weights and balance them between my thumb and fingers and do my nightly lifting. I still remember the smiling faces from nurses and doctors as they would peer into my room. I could only see them from the neck up, but I knew my lifting amused them.

As the day came to a close and the lights were turned off, I delved inward. I closed my eyes envisioning my spine as it had been, without a fracture or problem at all. I saw my damaged area and called for re-enforcements from my body to invade the damaged scar tissue and begin making pathways for my nerves to travel. I would see my nerves forcing their way through these newly opened lanes and traversing my spine. I would picture all my cells working furiously to make me whole again. I would then begin trying to move each and every lifeless part of my body. I would work my way from my waist, my legs, my ankles and eventually my toes. I could never see if I could ever move any of these parts, but it always felt as if I could move my toes. The nurses told me otherwise whenever I begged them to watch.

I could see on their face a painful expression. They could see no movement and I believe they never expected to. It was my insisting on them watching as I tried, that caused them pain. They thought I had unrealistic goals. They thought I was fooling myself with the optimism I had. I think they felt bad for me because they felt I didn't understand the seriousness of my situation. My mental focus along with my ability to meditate kept improving, like everything, it all gets better with practice. This was another gift I received from my accident, but this one I helped create myself. I became very good at deep, positive thoughts. I believe to this day I can do anything until proven otherwise. Many times I am proven otherwise, but without the attempt you'll never know your capabilities. Even when you do have a setback, be prepared to try again. Sometimes it's just a matter of preparation, practice, and persistence.

The rest of the night was a series of short naps interrupted by nurses coming in to turn me, waking up on my own, or the nightly routine. I longed to have the routine end early so that it would be behind me and would no longer be a concern for that night. Each time I awoke, I would fall asleep again meditating on healing.

I was dreaming constantly. Perhaps due to my disrupted sleep patterns I was just remembering them better. I was never disabled in these dreams. My dreams were always of me running, jumping and being the person I was before the accident. I loved these dreams. I wanted the real world to be the dream and my dream world to be real.

With each passing night my spasms were getting more and more intense. My legs would abruptly fly up off the bed, my stomach would inadvertently tighten up and sometimes my entire body would lock into a straightened position. I would ride out each experience until it passed. The doctors wanted me to take medications for my spasms, but I chose not to. Seeing my body move, whether by choice or not made me feel better, and even seemed to strengthen my hope to somehow beat this thing.

I prayed each night for a chance to coach again, a chance to teach again. I made an argument with the powers that be that I needed to recover enough so that I could resume my basketball and tennis coaching jobs as well as my summer tennis job. I said "I want to make a positive influence in other people's lives and a recovery of any degree would help me do that". I may not be religious, but I am a spiritual person who believes in a power stronger than my own. Meditation was my inner focus for my body healing itself.
Prayer was my outer focus on a superior being playing a part in my recovery. Working hard each day with the help from my therapists was my dedication. This was my recipe for health. This was my game plan for the future.

CHAPTER FIVE
Burning To Get Better

I noticed that as my spasms were increasing in frequency and in strength, my muscle tone was increasing as well. My stomach would seize up numerous times each hour, particularly during therapy and when lying down. It seemed any time my body was stretched into a new position my muscles would seize up. I would also spasm with stress, fear, excitement, etc... Extreme emotion would seem to always incite my body to go into spasms causing my muscles to tighten up much like a cramp. In my case, muscle cramps without any pain. It's amazing to see muscles that you can't voluntarily use tighten up and move body parts. I was in my fifth week since the injury and I had lost 40 pounds. I had lost mostly muscle and this was the lightest I had been since high school, so, adding whatever muscle mass I could was crucial.

The muscle spasms concentrated predominately in my stomach left me with a defined six-pack in my abdominals that was rather strange. I hadn't had such a defined stomach since my early twenties, yet I couldn't even lift a shoulder blade off the mat. A few times I was actually thrown out of my wheelchair from my stomach spasms. The therapists were pushing hard to get me on anti-spasm medication and I must admit, I did try them for a few days, but then opted to stop.

My doctors and nurses told me I had no control over my spasms, but they were wrong. They were definitely wrong. Some spasms occurred for no reason as far as I could tell but others did have a reason.

I was still fearful of many of the activities that were done during physical therapy. Reaching out for the cones and losing balance would trigger a spasm. Thinking of my accident triggered spasms. Stress triggered spasms. The after effects of the accident left me in a state in which the phone ringing unexpectedly sent shivers up my spine and sent me reeling with muscle contractions. I was still injured mentally. Although I felt I could control my mind and put myself in a relaxed state, I found myself afraid. I would tell myself that everything would be okay, but never could quite convince myself of that fact. My future was unsure regardless of how many times I told myself otherwise.

Spasms occurred throughout the day and though I couldn't alleviate the majority of them, I learned to control some of them. Each time I was in a stressful situation I would meditate and relax as best I could. When a spasm kicked in I became very good at riding it out and not fighting it. I was able to relax and concentrate on the area being affected. I may not have convinced the doctors, nurses or therapists, but this was a time when I was discovering my body, learning to listen to its every nuance and acting accordingly. I couldn't stop the spasms completely, but I knew how to cut down on the number and the severity of them. I knew spasms would help keep my muscles toned up and I needed them, but there needed to be a healthy balance. I couldn't let the spasms interfere with the work I wanted to accomplish.

One morning, Judy wanted to talk to me about my leg bag. My leg bag was strapped to my thigh with a tube leading to my penis and entering my bladder. Each day my leg bag would eventually fill and nurses would empty it as needed. Usually it would be emptied three times a day, and each time the nurse would write down the amount emptied into a journal.

When I was first admitted to Genesis I was asked if I'd be interested in a "Super Pubic". A Super Pubic is a permanent way to drain urine from the bladder by using an incision that would go directly into the bladder, bypassing the penis. Although I was tempted, I chose to pass on this option. I didn't want to do anything so permanent. I didn't want to burn any bridges that I didn't need to. I am very happy I chose not to go through with this operation. My expectations were higher than that. Judy now informed me of another option.

Judy wondered if I'd be interested in replacing the leg bag with catheterization. I was naïve and didn't understand exactly what she meant, so she explained. Three to four times a day I would have a catheter placed inside my penis. There are two types of catheters. One is a soft orange rubber and the other a stiff translucent made of what felt like plastic. I'm not sure why anyone would possibly choose to have the hard plastic rather than the soft rubber slid inside their genitals but I guess some do. The hard plastic did have one advantage. It was stiff and easy to manage. It could be slid inside the opening much easier than the softer orange one.

A catheter is just a small hollow tube with a slit opening in the front and a drainage opening on the other end. A catheter can be used for males or females.

I remember the first time watching Judy catheterize me. She explained what she was doing as she did it, in part to put me at ease and also to teach me for that time when I could do it on my own. She put on a new pair of plastic gloves and peeled back the wrapping from a new package containing a bright orange catheter. She then took a tube of lubricant and doused the tubing from top to bottom. She left the catheter in the package and grabbed the end that would stay outside my body and began twirling the catheter until lube was coating all sides. Judy then lifted the catheter out of the package.

The bed was raised and I was sitting up as she placed a plastic container between my knees and started working the gooey catheter into my penis. Finger over finger she gently worked the catheter deeper inside me. I could see the lube as it pooled at the opening. She made sure the other end of the catheter was sitting inside the plastic container between my knees. I was sure I could feel it as it slithered farther and farther inside me until finally a stream of yellow liquid started pouring into the container. The mind is an amazing thing. I probably couldn't feel a thing, but watching that tube enter such a fragile area I convinced myself I could.

The advantages of using a catheter are that you no longer have a bag full of urine connected to your leg and you also don't have a tube that can get caught and pulled (in my case yanked) accidentally. The down side of using a catheter is that it can be more time consuming, and even more importantly, can lead to increased infections in the bladder.

The bladder is vulnerable to outside microbes. Normally the bladder is a closed system, but microbes can easily migrate from hands and even the air and be taken in with the catheter. Microbes can then enter into the bladder and cause infection.

I decided to move away from the leg bag and start using the catheter. My hands were not able to manipulate the small catheters, so the nurses would have to catheterize me numerous times a day. I decided on the soft, orange ones by the way!

My strength was improving and my single pound weight turned to two, and soon I was able to begin working with weight machines in the therapy room. Each night I found myself lifting dumbbells until I was too tired to continue. I was able to move my wheelchair into the hallway and eventually start taking my chair to therapies on my own. It wasn't easy, but the sense of accomplishment that accompanied it was well worth it.

My lunch was from noon until one each day. I would eat my lunch in about fifteen minutes. I then had the rest of the time to do things I liked.

Sometimes my friend Mark would drop by with a tennis ball. He would roll me outside and throw a tennis ball to me from close range. Once I saw the ball coming I'd use both of my hands and basically crush it between my palms. I was very proud of how often I was able to catch that ball this way. The times I did catch that ball made it all worth it. Even if I never caught the ball it would have been worth it. Just to know that he would take time out of his own lunch hour to spend it with me meant a lot. I also loved the opportunity to be outside. I've always loved being outside, and since the accident nearly all of my time was spent inside.

One day Mark was able to stay a little longer. My occupational therapy was right after lunch and Mark stayed to watch. I was given two dimes and a nickel to put into a pop machine. It had to be painfully frustrating for Mark. I know it was for me. It had to be a good fifteen minutes before all the coins were in that machine. I would balance the coin in my fingers and then promptly drop it. Chrissie would pick it up and give it back to me and I'd try again. Sometimes, I would get the coin up to the slot, and then be encountered with the more difficult situation of getting it on end and holding it.

My fingers had trouble grasping the coin and so it usually fell to the ground when I tried. The purpose of all this was for me to learn to use my wrists to close my fingers. Try keeping your fingers relaxed, take your hand and hold it out in front of you with the wrist down, and notice how your fingers open up. Now slowly use your wrist to lift your hand and you'll notice your fingers, particularly the thumb and pointer finger coming together, this was the technique I'd be using to manipulate objects. I think it was a combination of luck and perseverance that got those three coins into that machine. I felt like a bit of a failure. I was trying to show off a bit since Mark was there. I think this exercise really brought to light to Mark and myself just how limited my abilities were up to this point.

I woke up in the middle of the night. My quadriceps, the muscles on the leg just above the knee, were burning furiously. My upper leg felt as though it were on fire; tingles of flames darting in and out of every pore. It could also be described as a swarm of bees descending upon my legs that were now stinging me continually. The sensation reminded me of heat. My legs were on fire and although it gave me discomfort, it didn't actually hurt. It was definitely difficult to sleep through. I really didn't know what to think about it, but I had the feeling it was a good thing. Even feeling discomfort was better than not feeling anything at all. These burning sensations in my lower extremities had me excited. It wasn't the type of feeling I was accustomed to before my accident

The next day in physical therapy I mentioned to Patty what had been going on. It was now 6 weeks from the date of my accident and my doctor had told me that if any feeling or movement were to come back it would happen in the first three weeks.

Patty took out a sharp pointed pin. She systematically poked me throughout my lower body each time asking if I could feel where she was. Although portions of my body still had no feeling, I was able to feel some of her pricks. The feeling was muted, as though through thick leather pants, but I definitely could feel something. She documented the test onto paper. I think Patty was as excited about this turn of events as I was. I mentioned to her the intense burning feeling I was having in both of my quadriceps. She wasn't quite sure what that was, if anything, but I could tell a spark was lit in her.

The burning continued to intensify in the coming days. I would lay in bed or on the mat and stare at the burning area. I would try moving my legs, but had little success. One night after supper and after the nurses had helped me to bed, I lay elevated in bed trying to lift my knee. My routine each night involved attempting to move each and every body part, focusing from each toe, foot, leg etc. It always ended with the same result: failure. I focused on my toes. I would focus on each toe individually and always ended with the same result: nothing. I tried to lift my knee, and nothing. I tried again and it appeared to move. It was incredibly slight, but it appeared to move. I tried again and again but noticed nothing, but on the third try it seemed to move again. I called in my nurse and told her "I think I moved my knee." She watched as I attempted to move it for her, but nothing happened. I was obsessed with making my knee move again. I was awake most of the night but couldn't seem to make it move. The staff eventually lowered the bed against my wishes and I eventually slipped off to sleep.

The next morning I called for a nurse and asked my bed be raised again. After numerous tries my knee finally moved. I waited until Judy, my assigned nurse, came in to start her day just before breakfast. I had Judy watch as I once again tried to move my knee and sure enough, it moved ever so slightly. She wasn't sure if it was voluntary or perhaps a convenient spasm masked as voluntary movement. She asked me to do it again, and I did. It moved about as much as a quiver on a cold winter's day, but it moved. I had something to work on. I knew I could turn this quiver into a quake. This was the best moment I had since I was admitted to rehab so long ago. My diminishing hope was renewed, and stronger than ever. The hardest part of the day was waiting until nine to tell Patty. I felt like a puppy having learned its first trick and bubbling over to show its' master.

I wheeled myself into the physical therapy room. It was a large open room where a handful of therapists worked. Looking around, there were already a few patients on mats beginning treatment. Most of the patients were older people having suffered debilitating strokes. There was one other spinal cord injured patient who had been recently admitted. His accident was also caused by a car crash.

His injury was at Cervical five. He breathed through tracheal tube coming out of his neck. He had a wife and a son. I had seen his little son running in the halls the past couple of days. It was sad to think that his life had been turned upside down, like my own, not to mention all the stroke victims trying to regain their life and hopefully their independence.

I couldn't help but think how his wife and son's life would be forever affected just by one simple mistake. I had seen him smoking a cigarette outside the previous night through his tracheal tube. I was taken aback. I thought to myself, "Wouldn't a tragedy like his make him think twice about smoking?" I then reasoned that perhaps most of what he enjoyed was taken away, just like me, and if he wanted to smoke it was his choice to make. I do have to admit there is just something strange about watching a person put a cigarette to a hole in their throat and watch the embers glow, later to see smoke bellow out from the same orifice.

Patty led me to our mat. I kept my secret concealed for the moment. She had me lay on my back as she stretched my achilles tendon, calves, hamstrings and so on.

Finally! While lying on my back I told her I had a surprise. My back propped up by pillows and legs laid out straight ahead I focused on my legs. I concentrated with all my might to make that knee move, but not even a budge. Patty asked what I was trying to do. I told her that yesterday I had repeatedly moved my knee. Not a lot, but enough that you could see it move upward a fraction of an inch. Patty took away all but one of the pillows propping up my back and head. The final pillow left my head just high enough so that I could see my knee in the bottom corner of my eye. I gritted my teeth, focused and tried again. This time it moved! Not only moved, but I raised my knee ¼ of an inch, farther than I had ever moved it the previous night!

I learned that body position plays a big part in the ability to move certain muscles. Sitting up fully made moving my knee much more difficult than laying flat on my back. I also soon learned that while wearing shoes I could only move my knee a quiver, but with my slippery socks on the mat I could raise my knee considerably more. My physical and occupational therapies were becoming a bit repetitive and this new found ability put a fresh twist on things.

For the following weeks Patty and Chrissie would innovate new tasks for me to attempt and practice. Patty decided to start working on my new found movement and see if we could make it stronger. Patty placed my foot in what was similar to a pair of roller skates, but the wheels were on the side of the skate rather than at the bottom. Lying on my side, Patty placed a slick board, somewhat like the board I used to transfer to and from my wheelchair only larger, below one of my legs. Lying in a fetal position, foot in skate atop the board, I would attempt to roll my leg along the board. I worked on this each day. In the beginning I was lucky to move my leg an inch, but as the days passed it increased until I could, with a good effort, move it across most of the board. I didn't have much control, I just gave it all I had and the leg would hopefully move. I found I was better at straightening my leg and not so good at bending it. Patty was going home and researching new tasks for me to do every night. She was a really good therapist who truly wanted to see me succeed.

It had been a week since that first moment I moved my knee. My mother was in my room. I lay on my back and made her cry by lifting my knee a few inches. I had to have my shoes off so that my socks could slide on the sheets of the bed, but I will always remember her tears. My mother was what I would term a "worrier". My accident devastated her. It was perhaps taking a bigger toll on her than me. It was nice to see her happy, though it may have been mixed feelings on her part. I mean, it was a long way off from walking.

Once again it took me to that movie "The Other Side of the Mountain" when the paralyzed skier asked her boyfriend to come into her room. He expected her to walk, but instead she was overjoyed at putting her clinched fist into a bag of potato chips and eventually pulling one out unbroken. But unlike Jill Kinmont, I didn't have to worry about my mother leaving my side like Kinmont's boyfriend did. My mother was a lovely, caring soul who would have done anything for me, and wished she could. I know she would have traded places with me given the chance.

That evening I had a long talk with my wife Cindy. My ability to move my legs and the hopes of moving more had her looking at other rehabilitation clinics.

The second highest rated Rehab Clinic in the country was a place called RIC or Rehabilitation Institute of Chicago. Chicago was only 170 miles from where I was currently.

I hated leaving my nurses and therapists, especially Patty, who had done so much for me. I also knew that I would see a lot less of my daughter and my family. I couldn't expect to have visitors every night like I was used to, but it was a move I felt I needed to do. RIC had much more experience with spinal cord patients. They had more facilities. It was obvious that a change was a good idea, not because my treatment was inferior, but that there, treatment would be even better. That was my hope, so the decision was made and I was off to Chicago.

CHAPTER SIX
Off to R.I.C. in Chicago

Cindy made arrangements to take me to Chicago. She came with a friend of hers who owned a Ford Escort very similar to the one I was in when I had my accident. They parked in the rear parking lot, gathered up my things from the room and wheeled me outside. I had been practicing the past few weeks transferring into a beat up shell of a car that was in the PT room. Transferring into a car is no easy feat when wearing a full Halo and vest. Since it's impossible to bend from the waist to the tip of your head, it's a challenge finding a way through a car door. A person wearing a Halo must lean heavily in numerous directions to work the upper body through the opening. Couple that with a complete lack of stomach muscles and weak arms and a seemingly easy maneuver becomes quite challenging. The key was finding places to put your hands to either lean or push off of. I had been practicing transferring into that car, but I always needed help and this was no exception. I did improve enough to at least help in the whole process.

The transfer was done with the help of Cindy, her friend, and to some extent, myself. It wasn't quick, it wasn't pretty, but eventually I was sitting upright in the front passenger seat, the bolts from my Halo just inches from the roof of the car. Cindy and her friend then went to the rear of the car to start loading up all my belongings. As they left, Cindy's friend reached back and closed my passenger side door. As the door clicked shut, I felt a tug against my body. My head was being dragged backward and with it my entire body. When it finally came to a stop I was locked in tightly to the back of the seat. My head tilted back as far as possible. I was unable to move.

With a shallow, creaky voice I yelled for help but the combination of my paralyzed diaphragm and my vocal cords still in repair, a whispery sound was all I could seem to muster. The two women were busy talking amongst themselves as they loaded the car, and I was forced to patiently wait as they loaded each item. When finished Cindy jumped in the back seat and her friend behind the wheel.

In a kind, but desperate voice I asked her "Can you please open my door?" I'm still not sure how neither one of them noticed instantly that I had a problem. My body from the waist up was tilted back and tight against the back of the seat. I was staring at the roof of the car motionless. I felt as though I was in the advanced stages of rigor mortis. The driver was the first to notice my dilemma. She yelled "Oh my God!" and then Cindy noticed as well. The driver jumped out of her seat, ran around the front of the car, grabbed the handle to my door and flew it open. The automatic chest restraint disengaged and I was released from my bondage. After some close scrutiny, Cindy and her friend discovered what had caused my momentary plight. The bolt to my Halo that sticks straight up from my head had inadvertently slid into the track that guided the automatic chest restraint. As the restraint engaged it dragged my Halo along the track to the back of my seat and locked me in. They dislodged the bolt from the track and closed the door. We all laughed for quite a while. I mean, what the heck else can go wrong? It wasn't a big deal, no injuries, and it gave us a good laugh for most of our trip.

It was a very long three and a half hour drive to the Rehabilitation Institute of Chicago. They had my door locked and had me leaning against the door. It was much the same way you'd put some fragile, somewhat breakable object in with you. I was kind of tucked into the corner, leaning against the side of the door to make sure I didn't fall over and break. Three and a half hours is a long time when you can't adjust your position. No one was happier than me when we finally parked. Through much trial and error I found myself outside the vehicle and back into my wheelchair. I say "my wheelchair," but it was actually a loaner from the hospital. Cindy would return it when she went back and I would get a different wheelchair from RIC.

RIC is a large place with many floors. Spinal cord patients were on the seventh floor, but first we had to check in at the front desk. One of the therapists gave us a quick tour of the various parts of the facility I'd be using each day and then I was taken to my new room.

I had my own room, and a very spacious one, at Genesis West. Genesis West was a hospital that did rehabilitation. This was a Rehabilitation Center that did some minor hospital work. This center only dealt with minor health issues. Northwest Hospital was right next door and you could reach it without ever stepping outside. In case of major health issues you'd be transferred there. I would be sharing my new room with three other patients. There were approximately one hundred patients at the facility, and rooms were limited.

It was Tracy who led us to my room. There was one other patient in the room at the time. My room was in the back right corner. The walls that separated my corner from the rest of the room consisted of a fabric curtain that draped on a circular rod around my bed. Tracy was one of the head therapists on the seventh floor. She was well versed in working with spinal cord patients and the first thing she wanted to do was get me into bed and off my butt. I usually tried to avoid the bed, but I was anxious to lie down. The trip had worn me out and I knew from the teachings at Genesis West that it was important to get off my butt from time to time. It had been more than five hours since I had given my body a break. I sure didn't want complications from sores slowing me down now. I was positioned on my side with pillows stuffed against my back and butt so I wouldn't accidentally roll onto my back. I stayed like this for a couple hours while Tracy took Cindy and her friend to their room for the night.

The seventh floor had a room for visitors and Cindy had reserved it for them. They would be staying just down the hall from me. When that room was full, they would make arrangements with visitors to stay at the local Ronald McDonald house. RIC did what they could to help not only their patients, but also the patient's family.

It was getting later into the evening and I was in for a treat. Tracy removed the pillows from my bed and put me on my back. She began pulling the Velcro away from my woolen lined vest.

It had been about a month since this vest was put on and it had never been removed. The inside looked like fluffy cream wool and I can only imagine how much it must have itched against my skin these past few weeks, that is if I could have felt it.

Tracy was ripping at my vest like a mad woman. Each pull set off a loud crackle as the two Velcro straps separated from each other. I was able to stop her for a moment just to make sure she knew what she was doing. The previous hospital wouldn't have dreamt of taking off this vest for any reason. She was tearing it off like a ravenous person ripping into a candy bar. Moments later she had the vest disconnected from my Halo, my bare chest seeing the light of day for the first time in over a month. She undressed me and transferred me onto a shower chair. She placed a towel across my waist.

Tracy took me to the mirror. My body had wasted away. The muscles from my chest were gone. I was thinner than I had ever seen myself. The only tone I had was from my stomach where a constant barrage of spasms had formed a tidy six-pack. I had no body fat, just bones, skin, and those six little lumps in my abdomen. I couldn't help but think how much had changed in my life in just over a month. My body looked like it had never jogged a mile, had never run the length of a basketball court or never hit a tennis ball. My reflection reminded me of the posters you sometimes see asking for donations for the starving people around the world. It's hard to describe how I felt right then. I was disappointed. I was sad. Sometimes "out of sight out of mind" isn't such a bad thing.

Tracy had medium length brown hair that curled at the ends. She was in great shape and looked like she worked out. She was extremely sweet and caring. She was someone you liked almost immediately, always smiling and positive. She wheeled me over to the shower and removed the towel from my lap. She turned the water on and adjusted the temperature. When she felt the water was right she wheeled me under the flowing stream of water.

When I was a freshman in High School I was on the freshman basketball team. Our school had a rule that all basketball players received a crew cut. My hair was somewhat long and covered my ears, getting a crew cut was a drastic change. One thing I remember the most was that first time I took a shower. I could feel the water droplets crashing against my now bare scalp for the first time.

It was a weird sensation, feeling the temperature and the impact of each one of those hurdling drops. It's a memory that has stuck with me all my life.

When Tracy wheeled me into the shower, a similar but somewhat different sensation happened. The water began striking my naked body. I could feel the warm water as it bounced off my skin giving me a wonderful and soothing sensation that I hadn't felt for over a month. This sensation was limited to just above my chest. Below my shoulders I couldn't feel the water or its accompanying warmth. I could see the water as it hit me but I felt nothing. It was surreal. I had some feeling in particular areas below my chest, but only when accompanied with pressure. My ability to feel temperature was completely non-existent.

Tracy used a washcloth with soap and washed my entire body. She gave Cindy a lesson on how to bathe me. Showers were a special deal that didn't happen all the time at RIC. I would receive a shower several times a month while my Halo was on, and it was usually Tracy who bathed me.

I slept better that night than I had since my accident. Maybe it was the bathing, the exhausting trip, or perhaps the new bed, but it felt amazing to get the rest. I forgot what it felt like to feel good. I didn't really wake up completely even when staff interrupted me during the night. The morning found me refreshed. I felt strong and ready for the next challenge. The nursing portion of my care would be much less intensive here at RIC. I would still get repositioned during the night, but less often. Some medications would change. They eliminated the Colace that was stimulating my bowels and turning my excrement into a broth similar to a thin soup. RIC had a new and much different way of extracting waste products from my body and I would learn all about it in the coming days and weeks.

Genesis, as I mentioned earlier, was primarily a hospital with excellent nurses and healthcare. Genesis used medications that kept my bowels in a liquid state. The drugs Colace would liquefy and Senokot would keep things moving along. A suppository at bedtime insured that everything would come to fruition sometime during the night. I must admit, there were a few times during my stay at Genesis that this didn't work as planned.

I remember twice having accidents during the middle of the day. One day, having just had my lunch fed to me, I began wheeling down the hallway trying to kill time and strengthen my arms before therapy.

My stomach began hurting and though my sense of feeling was severely impaired I could feel the explosion. Liquid goo filled my pants and rolled down my legs. Nurses don't get paid enough for cleaning up situations like this.

I tried my very best to keep positive thoughts, but it'd be a lie if I told you moments like this didn't take it's toll on my psyche. I felt absolutely horrible. I felt helpless and a loser. I questioned my worth. I would spend the rest of the day with a sad and heavily burdened heart. Maybe it's just my own hang up, but incontinence bothered me intensely. I would need to look at things differently and not beat myself up over this. With each step forward, incidences like this took me two steps back. I really couldn't afford to go backwards because I still had such a long way to go.

Suppositories were more of a last resort at RIC. They had their own system that was equally effective. It involved less drugs, but my Senokot remained a mainstay. Recovery from a spinal cord injury can be looked at in stages, each stage pushing the body forward with the ultimate goal of being independent, while striving to return to where you once were.

It's important to focus on the journey that takes you toward your goal, rather than focusing too intensely on just the goal. Each injury has it's limitations or lack thereof. Focusing on a goal that is ultimately unattainable can do harm mentally. Follow the path leading towards recovery, stay on it and work hard to keep moving forward. If you reach your destination, that is amazing. If not, appreciate how far down the path you've traveled, and how much closer you are to your destination than had you decided to sit down and go nowhere.

To sum it up more simply, I may never play sports again, but if I can pick up my two year old daughter and carry her around on my lap, then all this will be worth it. If I can only hug her, well, that's amazing too! I will try to be happy with whatever I can attain because aren't we all truly going for the same thing? Happiness!

From this point on, I would no longer be groomed to expel my wastes on a bed pad in the middle of the night. The plan at RIC is to take care of all that before you go to sleep. Senokot is a wonder drug as far as I'm concerned. It worked well for me. It keeps things moving along even for a person in my condition whose body can't help the process.

The combination of Senokot and the use of what they referred to as "Digis-tim" helped me complete my nightly ritual and move my bowels each day.

I eventually got clearance to move my bowels every other day. Before my accident I probably moved my bowels once every three or four days, so trying to get something out of me each and every day seemed like quite the stretch. Every other day seemed like a good compromise to appease their protocols and allow me a peaceful night off. If I had my way, it'd be every four days, but that idea seemed to freak them out a bit. I was given the speech about the toxicity of bowels left in the body too long, so a compromise was in order. Wonder what they would have thought had I told them that before my accident I moved my bowels every four days and sometimes longer.

Digistim, as they called it, was my least liked activity at RIC. Sur-rounding your anus is the anus sphincter, and comprising the anus sphincter are the puborectalis muscles. The puborectalis muscles play a large part in initiating bowel movements.

This is how Digistim is done. The nurse puts on gloves and inserts a finger into the anus. Using a circular motion, the nurse begins massaging the area around the sphincter, thereby relaxing the puborectalis muscles and hopefully stimulating the body to push out the bowels. This method works very well, but isn't foolproof. When digistim didn't work, I would normally be given a suppository and the whole process would be repeated again some time later.

The nursing staff was relentless. They were going to get that crap out of me if it was the last thing they did. They had to document my bowel movements as well as the amount of urine drained from catheterization. This was one of their highest priorities. It's dangerous to store up too much waste for too long of a time, and it can even kill you. Bladders that become too full can overflow into the kidneys and cause kidney damage. I was constantly being told what a fragile precipice I was balancing on. I wasn't one who lived my life dwelling on my own fragility, but they caused me to evaluate my health more closely. The whole process encouraged me to become more in tune with my body. Not to over dramatize each ache and pain, but to recog-nize when my body was trying to tell me something. I become more aware. My paralysis made it more difficult to hear the whispers of my body trying to tell me something, so I had to learn to listen all that much more closely.

The body also has its' own built in warning signs when something isn't going quite right. It's an autonomic reaction the body sends out to warn the person of a problem. When I had a problem, my spasms (Spasticity) would increase and many times I would break into a sweat. At this time in my recovery I wasn't in tune with my body enough to detect these symptoms and tie it into a potential problem, but in time I would be able to detect them immediately. By detecting these autonomic warnings and acting to correct the problems, I would avert some major health problems in my life in the coming years.

I woke up my first morning at RIC. I looked at the curtains drawn around my bed. It seemed the hustle and bustle of the morning crew preparing to make their rounds might have stirred me from my sleep. It was only a matter of minutes before voices could be heard entering my room and the curtains were being drawn back. Standing in front of me was a nurse and a doctor. The nurse's name was Jennifer, whom I will refer to as just Jen. Jen had dark brown hair that flowed down to her shoulder blades. Her locks were thick with just a slight curl. Her face was kind and beautiful. She had brown eyes and olive colored skin. Jen was short, perhaps five foot two or so. I would find out in time that she was very kind, giving and extremely knowledgeable and professional at her job. She was to be my primary nurse. The doctor was also somewhat short and stood perhaps five foot five or so. He had short black hair and was of Chinese descent. He had a rounded face and was very businesslike when he spoke. He was referred to as Dr. Wang. They introduced themselves and described their role at the facility. They outlined what I should expect in the upcoming days and weeks. When they had finished they strolled out together. It felt a bit like that first day of school when you're just trying to figure out everything; that feeling of excitement in meeting all new people, but the slight terror of it all too. I was not quite sure what to expect next.

Now that the curtains were drawn back, I had full view of my room. There were four beds, each resting in the four corners of the room. The two beds on the left side of the room were empty. I was in the bed at the back right, and in the bed at the front right was another patient.

I looked over in his direction. He was lying on his back, eyes closed. He didn't have a Halo, but did have a heavy brace on his back that I would later find out was called a "Turtle Shell". I was looking in his direction wondering what horrible disaster befell him. His face just didn't seem to look right. He had bulging eyeballs, one of which was so pronounced it looked like it may fall out completely. His skin seemed charred on his face and even on his hands. He was able to walk on his own and soon he got himself dressed and walked out of the room without glancing over or saying a word. Minutes later, Jen stopped back in and helped me get my clothes on. She and another nurse helped me into my chair without bothering to use a sliding board. They positioned my feet, and with a tug, moved me the foot or so from my mattress to my wheelchair. They wheeled me out into the hall and into a world I couldn't have possibly imagined. This was a world that everyone who complains over trivial things should see. A world that can't help but make you appreciate all you have. My new world was filled with people whose problems far outweigh those you would normally encounter in a day.

My room was only a few doors away from the cafeteria area that I would eat in three times a day for the next several months. It was a gathering point for people who all had horrific stories that led them to this place. All with hopes like mine that they might somehow escape this nightmare. When we would get together for meals though, you'd never know just how much our lives had changed. We still laughed. We enjoyed each others' company and smiled. Even when altered drastically, life continues to go on.

Jen wheeled me up to a table and asked me what I'd like to eat. My meals here were much simpler than they were at Genesis. Here my typical morning meal would consist of cereal. I was proud of the fact I had figured out a way of intertwining the handle of the spoon between my fingers and could eat without the aid of devices on my fingers. I still dropped my spoon often, and I tended to make a mess, but I could eat my cereal and free up nurses to help others who needed help much more than me.

After eating my cereal, I began glancing around. This was a big room and it was filled with patients. I had never seen a person paralyzed from the neck down and now I was looking at many of them. Some were in regular wheelchairs that were pushed by attendants and others were chairs that were controlled by blowing into a straw.

The wheelchairs fitted with a straw were big heavy electric wheelchairs. The straw would stick out just to the tip of the lips. The person in the wheelchair would grab the straw with his/her lips and through a series of blows be able to move the chair forward, backward, and make turns. Some seemed to have this mastered and tooled around with ease, while others were a disaster about to happen. They reminded me of the first time I drove a stick shift; the sudden accelerations followed by intermittent abrupt stops. You wouldn't want one of these large, heavy behemoths to ever run over your feet. Nurses and attendants kept clear when an inexperienced straw driver was coming through!

The table I was sitting at had a wide variety of injuries. Nearly everyone had some sort of spinal cord injury, but some were very high, like those paralyzed from the neck down and some much lower. These people pushed their own chairs, ate without help and required far less help. I was somewhere in the middle. There were plenty of people with injuries similar to mine. Breaking the lower part of the neck is one of the most common types of spinal cord injury.

I talked to a black man who sat across from me. His name was Chuck and he was about ten years older than me. He was a little overweight, but wore a grin on his face and seemed genuinely happy all the time. He was a police officer in Chicago and got shot in his lower back while trying to apprehend a suspect in a crime. He had been at RIC for a couple of months and was going to be leaving soon. I would get to know Chuck better in the coming days, but it was time for my class, and Jen was all over it.

CHAPTER SEVEN
Therapy in Chicago Begins

Jen gave me a schedule of my classes and pulled me out from the table. She rolled me down the hallway to the elevators. One side of the elevators had attendants running them and the other side was for those who could push the buttons themselves. I was capable of using either side. There were many floors to RIC. I was currently on the seventh, but there were more above. My therapies would be primarily confined to three separate floors.

The floor just below mine was the sixth floor. It was the pediatric floor. The entire floor was dedicated to children from horrific accidents or other debilitating circumstances that caused them to need help. Jen pushed me into an elevator, made sure the right button was pushed, and then stepped out. I was on my own. I knew the floor and my new therapist's name. My new physical therapist was Kate.

The elevator opened and I pushed my chair out the door. There was a large waiting area where numerous people in wheelchairs had gathered. Some were by themselves, while other people were accompanied by an attendant. We all had ten more minutes before our scheduled appointments, so I found an open area to sit and wait.

I was patiently waiting when I saw a very young girl being wheeled in by an attendant. She was a young black girl, probably no more than six years old. She was in a small wheelchair made for a girl her size. The first thing I saw as she got pushed alongside me was this beautiful, monster sized smile on her face. The woman pushing the young girl into the waiting area had a huge smile as well. They rolled across the room and it seemed everyone in the room knew this young girl.

Patients and therapists were all greeting her with words like, "Hi, Angel" and she replied to each therapist by using their first name. She had obviously been there awhile and was undoubtedly loved very much. She had this amazing glow to her that was addictive. I found myself wearing a huge grin myself as I watched her rolling nearer to my chair. She had an inner happiness that warmed your heart.

The young girl was small, even for a six year-old. She had severe burns over most of her body. Her arms were covered in loose red and white skin that was scarred throughout. The right side of her face was the same with no discernable skin left other than the scar tissue that now hung to her face with a rough texture of rolling mounds. The left side of her face had scars as well, but she retained most of her natural skin. I saw nothing but beauty when I looked at her, but I'm sure there are those that would have seen her outward appearance and thought quite the opposite.

I looked at her spirit and felt warmth fill my heart. If I ever felt sorry for my own situation before, this was a wake up call. How can a person possibly feel bad for themselves when they see a beautiful young girl who has barely lived need a wheelchair to get around. And yet she shone like a bright light, spreading her joy to everyone around her. She was amazing.

I talked to her briefly before she was taken in for her appointment. I felt as though I was talking to an adult yet she was only a child. She had an older soul and her huge smile never left her face. It made me wonder where she got all this courage. Where could she have attained all this maturity? I wondered if re-incarnation was real. She seemed to have inherited this incredible spirit from a very wise and beautiful soul. Perhaps she was chosen for this task because of the trials she would need to endure. Nothing has ever touched me more than how this little girl handled her situation.

She would only be at RIC for the rest of the week. When Friday came, each and every therapists came out to give her a big hug and say good-bye. I can't speak for the other patients but I had tears creeping down my cheek. I was going to miss this young girl, but the strength she had given me would last the rest of my life.

In the coming months I was told what had happened to her. Her mother had beaten her. She had beaten her so bad that she ended up breaking her back, causing her spinal cord damage and resulting in paralysis. Her mother then poured gasoline over her and lit her on fire in the hopes of covering up the situation. Somehow, the little girl survived, and her mother was now in prison.

After hearing this, it made it even more amazing that she could live life with such a zest; always wearing that big smile. To see her living her life with happiness, even when she had been betrayed by the person who should love her the most. I hope she remained happy after leaving the safe confines of RIC. I wonder if the environment at RIC was so much better than what she had been accustomed to growing up. I have a feeling deep in my heart that she wasn't excited to leave all the therapists and nurses that she had grown so close to.

I prayed for her after she left. I pray that she lives with people that care for her. I pray that she is loved and I pray that people in this world see the beautiful person she is and not the physical deformities that she must live with the rest of her life. Angel, I hope you live a long and happy life and that you continue spreading that beautiful joy that overflows from your heart!

An athletic girl with short blonde hair asked me if I was Dave. "I'm Kate" she said, "I'll be your Physical Therapist". She asked me if I could push my own chair. I replied "yes," and I followed her into the next room. She helped me take my shoes off and we transferred onto the mat. Once again, a transfer board was not used. She wrapped a gait belt around my waist and positioned my feet. Working together, she grabbed my gait belt, pulled up, and pulled me over to the mat. I fell onto my back and she helped me into a sitting position. "Do you have any sensation below your injury line?" she asked. The injury line is the line across my upper chest that separates the area that is paralyzed from the area that isn't. "Yes," I said. She walked away and came back with all the tools she needed to test my ability to feel. Much like Patty had done at Genesis, she went from body part to body part, testing my sensation of feeling. I could tell my ability to detect sensation had improved since the previous test, but I still had trouble feeling some of the pinpricks, especially when she got to my feet.

My ability to feel had been improving over the past couple of months. It was different than before the accident, but it was great just to know I could feel something. It still felt as though I was wearing heavy leather pants over my skin that deadened the sensation of touch. I still couldn't feel pain below my line. The outer sensitivity of my skin was dull, but I could feel pressure; even the slight pressure from the end of a pin. I didn't feel every pinprick, but I could sense the majority of the ones in my stomach and thighs. As she went down my body the sensation became less and less until she reached my feet. My feet were so numb you probably could cut them off and I wouldn't have noticed.

Kate was tall. She looked to be about 6 foot or so. She was attractive in a tomboy kind of way. She was easily the strongest of any of my therapists and she was very motivated. She was like having a great coach. A physical therapist is a coach in my opinion, but their coaching is far more important than mere sports. Her ability to bring the best out of me, would affect my future and the way I would live. I was fortunate to have Kate. She was going to push me much like Patty had, only here she had access to many more tools to help make my recovery happen.

After each test with her pin she would write down whether I had sensation or not. She documented each body part onto a form. I would be tested periodically and these forms would be compared and checked for improvement.

My hour with Kate had ended and I was off to the elevators again, heading to occupational therapy with a Melissa. I was on time, and soon Melissa walked over and introduced herself. Melissa had short blonde hair. Very blonde, perhaps dyed blonde. I think the term used is "Platinum" blonde. Her hair curled under just below the ears. She was very thin and medium height. She had deep blue eyes and light, pale skin. She looked as if she were frail, but I would soon find out she was stronger than she appeared. She spent our first hour evaluating my abilities, in particular my hands. She laid my hands in her palm and straightened, pulled, and rubbed each individual finger. She then manipulated my hands and wrists. Her goal was to help me become independent with my everyday needs such as dressing, showering, toiletry, and so on. Her main focus would be to improve my hand function, maintain my stretching, and overlapping with Kate, improve my lower body.

Therapy on the first day was somewhat uneventful. It reminded me of going to school on that first day when the teacher tries to get to know everyone's name. You might get a syllabus or your books, but you don't really learn anything and are almost never given homework. My first day in therapy was meeting my therapists, having my condition evaluated, and them creating a game plan from that information. I only had five hours of therapy this first day, and I finished early and went back to my room until dinner.

My roommate was in the room and I finally got a chance to talk to him. His name was Greg. Greg had dark red hair that was coarse and thick. His hair was curly and of medium length. He had a light complexion dotted with red freckles. He was stocky and of medium height. He looked Scottish to me. His eyes bulged out abnormally. One was so bad that it looked like it was about to fall out of its' socket. He had a circle on his head that was blackened and lacked hair as if burnt. He could walk, but there was a noticeable limp. Limp may not be the best way to describe it, but when he walked you could tell it was strained and looked unnatural.

Greg had worked for an electrical company. He had been called to work on a power outage. He had scaled an electrical pole in full gear and was working near a transformer when he came in contact with a live wire, which sent huge amounts of electricity flowing through his head, exiting near his feet. The jolt threw him from the pole. The electricity caused his eyes to bug out and left him with severe nerve damage. The nerve damage was why he couldn't seem to walk right. His walk was jerky and forced. He told me he had been at RIC for six weeks and was getting discharged in a couple of days. I never got the chance to get to know Greg that well. He kept to himself and didn't talk unless he was spoken to, but he was a very nice guy whom my heart went out to.

I was reminded of one of my favorite animated Christmas stories, "Rudolph The Red Nosed Reindeer", the version where the elf wants to be a dentist. They get caught on an iceberg and travel to the Island of Misfit Toys. I felt I was now on the Island of Misfit Toys where each person had a tragic story, and each tragic story ended with them arriving here.

Dinner was a family type event. I sat across from Chuck, the policeman, and a friend of his named Kevin. Kevin interested me because he was about my age and had an injury like mine. I could tell that his disability was very similar.

His hands were a little better, and could hold silverware better than me, but many of his problems were mine as well. He was injured about a month before I was. After recovering his health in the hospital he was taken directly here to RIC. I watched him eat his food and imagined my own hands improving to his level in the coming months.

I ate my food without the help of anyone. I would drop my utensils constantly, but I would pick them back up and continue. I would still need help from time to time, but I wanted to do things on my own. I would meet many people at dinner this first week, some who thought like me and tried to do things on their own, and others who preferred to have others help them. I am not going to judge what others do, but for me, getting as little help as possible forced me to find my own ways of getting things done. It was almost a selfish thing. I didn't like relying on anyone else. I wanted to rely on myself.

I met a young man in his late teens that was a C-6. I was basically a C-6 to C-7, though I also broke C-5 as well. His disability was similar to mine. We both could use our biceps, but are triceps were weak and partially paralyzed. This young man's name was Matt, and he was never without his mother. His mother came every day and followed him through his therapy. She helped him with everything he did, from eating to getting in and out of his chair. You could see the pain in her face as she interacted with her son. She would help him get through every day. The toll of his injury was written all over her face. I thought, at the time, that she may have felt guilt for his injury, but he, like so many of the people here, became injured as a result of a motorcycle accident. I mention Matt as a point of comparison. We were both injured at approximately the same time, yet I was capable of doing so much more for myself. I suppose if you know you will have a person helping you throughout your life it becomes a matter of choice. Maybe I don't want to be in a position that I can't control. I guess I trust myself more than I trust other people. Whatever the reason, I continued to only ask for help when I had no other choice, and Matt chose to have things done for him. We were both happy, and I enjoyed Matt's company very much.

After the first week, my wife Cindy and I were able to convince the powers at RIC to give me a full eight-hour day. I would start at eight in the morning and finish at five in the evening with a one-hour lunch at noon. I maintained my motivation, but was exhausted at the end of each day.

CHAPTER EIGHT
A New Way to Think

Some of the classes that were added to my schedule included a strengthening class and a wheelchair class. In the wheelchair class we did numerous activities involved with getting around in our wheelchairs. Two guys were in charge of the wheelchair class. They reminded me of the guys I used to play basketball with at the University of Iowa when I lived in Coralville. They were strong, fit, and in their twenties. They both appeared quite athletic. If I sound like a broken record when describing people as athletic, I think it's because so many of the therapists took really good care of themselves.

We were a group of about seven or eight guys in wheelchairs. There were no women. Not as many women suffer spinal cord injuries as men, at least not from my experience. Whatever the reason, it was all guys and no girls. We had two therapists and a number of volunteers that varied from day to day.

We would gather in our homeroom and then head towards the elevators, take them to the first floor, and out the door. It was such a treat to smell the fresh air and feel the sun's warmth on my face. I had been indoors nearly all the time and when I did get outside it was after my therapies. I would eat dinner and by the time I got outside, the sun was setting or it was all ready dark. Passing through the front doors and onto the sidewalk brought the sight of wheelchairs everywhere. Patients were smoking cigarettes, while others seem to be waiting for someone. Still others just seemed to be appreciating another beautiful day in Chicago.

My chair here at RIC had push rims that were round. These rims were the typical push rims you usually see on a chair, smooth and round. I no longer had projection rims that had knobs sticking out.

My push rims were covered with a rubber type material to give me better grip. My hands weren't capable of holding onto the rims, so I used friction by pressing my hands against the rubbery surface. This class was designed for Paraplegics, and I was the only Quadriplegic in the class. We would head out to various destinations, and today we were headed to Navy Pier on the shores of Lake Michigan.

We started our journey as a group, but as our journey continued, some were quicker than others and soon our group became scattered. I realized immediately how much weaker I was than the rest of the class. I was so caught up in the improvements I'd been making that I forgot just how impaired I still was. I couldn't compete with someone who had full arm strength and hand movement. They were capable of going far faster than me, and soon they were leaving me in their dust. I tried the best I could to keep up by myself, but I must admit, a volunteer needed to give me intermittent pushes just to keep me in contact with the group.

I never realized how much sidewalks are slanted until then. Sidewalks are slanted towards the road so that rain can drain off and into the sewers. When walking it makes little difference, but when pushing a wheelchair it makes a huge difference. It becomes a constant battle to keep a straight line and not let gravity take your chair straight into the road. The arm closest to the street is working as hard as it can, while the opposite arm is hardly working at all. This is what happens when you're on a slant. My right arm was much stronger than my left. I soon learned that I wanted to be on the left side of the street, where my right arm would be closest to the road and do most of the work. I still spent some time on the right side of the road just because my left arm needed to get stronger, but I could never keep up with the group from that side and always needed some help from my volunteer attendant.

We would travel to many places. When we were at Navy Pier we traveled to various shops, checked out the pier and Lake Michigan, and just enjoyed the sites. We would also travel to the "Miracle Mile" and practice opening and closing doors by entering the many stores that lined the streets. The therapists would take us to places where there were hills and ramps to climb.

We got many stares from people not expecting to see seven or eight guys in wheelchairs traveling about. I was used to getting stares. A Halo makes a person look so much like Frankenstein that people couldn't help but take a look.

One day, in our therapy room, the therapists brought out an elevated platform made of wood that simulated a street curb. We gathered in a circle with our wheelchairs as they explained what needed to be done to properly jump a curb. Afterward, the therapists walked around and removed our tip bars. Tip bars work a lot like training wheels, but while training wheels keep a bike from falling on it's side, tip bars are designed to keep the chair from tipping over backwards. The policy for RIC was to keep tip bars on the back of wheelchairs, but this limited what you could do in a wheelchair. You can't jump curbs with tip bars on. Believe me, I've tried. What usually happens when you try to jump a curb with tip bars is you end up with the front wheels above the curb and the tip bars below, causing the two large side wheels to be elevated off the ground, you can't go forward or backward because you just spin your wheels.

The therapist made jumping curbs look easy. Squaring the chair directly at the curb, pushing the chair at a somewhat high rate of speed, then just as the front wheel is about to hit the curb, leaning back, giving the push rim a hard push. The front wheel pops into the air and the large side wheels slam into and over the curb. Piece of cake!

We took turns attacking this elevated platform. There were some successes and many failures. Finally it was time for me to give it a go. I lined up my chair with the curb and took off as fast I could. Just as I reached the platform I leaned back and pushed the rims as hard as I could. The platform was about four inches above the ground and my front wheel elevated about two inches. With a thud, my front wheels slammed into the wood and my chair came to an abrupt stop.

We took turns for the entire hour. I had about twenty attempts, and I did make it a couple times. The majority of my failures came about like the first by not getting my wheelie high enough. I tried slowing down and this enabled me to get my front wheels high enough to clear the front of the curb, but then my speed wouldn't carry my side wheels up and over the curb, which caused the chair to flip over backward.

Luckily, therapists followed us on every attempt and when we flipped over they caught us. We also practiced holding wheelies and pushing our chair while keeping the front wheels off the ground.

There are so many obstacles in the real world when you're in a wheelchair. Places without elevators, doors that aren't wide enough, curbs, steps... the list goes on and on. Learning how to jump curbs, learning to hold the front wheels up and still push your chair, takes some of these obstacles away. As time went on we would learn how to climb steps and how to go down steps. The feeling of fear still had a tendency to set off spasms. I remember the fear as I headed off at full speed, attempting to jump three successive platforms that simulated steps. I felt the fear of flipping over and then my stomach locked up and spasms would throw me forward. Without a lap belt I would have been sprawling around on the floor.

One big difference between RIC and Genesis is RIC was willing to take more chances to prepare us for the outside world. Safety is important, but too much safety isn't realistic. You can't live in a fantasy world and then expect to handle the real world. Sometimes hospitals are so caught up with sheltering themselves from any potential lawsuits that they limit the growth of the patient. RIC was aggressive. They weren't careless, but they pushed the patients to do as much as they could on their own. A good example of taking therapy to a high level happened in this very class just a week after Thanksgiving.

We pushed our chairs into a shopping mall within the "Miracle Mile". We met near the escalators. Therapists took us one by one up the moving stairs. Patients rolled onto the stairs backwards, locked their chairs, and grabbed tightly to the moving side rails. Once the chair is near the top, you unlock the chair, lean forward and push the chair off. If you didn't let go of the rail and lean forward the chair would come to the end of the escalator, where walkers would normally step off, and the chair would flip over back-wards. This is particularly bad because as you lay on your back floundering, people on the escalator are still coming and have no way to get around you. I can speak from experience what a mess this can cause, as I would try it again at an airport in about fifteen years.

I was the last one to go, and it was probably because I was the only one that was Quadriplegic and had major problems with my hands.

I wheeled backwards and snapped on both of my brakes. The stairs caught my chair. As I rose, my chair tilted heavily forward. I was strapped to my chair with a belt and had my hands on the moving rail. There were therapists in front of me and behind me. I held on to that rail with all my might. I felt like my chair and I were about to tumble forward and roll down the steps, and I was fighting to keep this from happening. There was a time, as I ascended, I felt everything was under control. Now it was just a matter of reaching the top. Upon reaching the top I clicked off the brakes, leaned forward and pushed my chair off the platform. It was quite a rush. I have a feeling it was quite a rush for the therapists too. This wasn't exactly the type of thing I envisioned doing in the future. It seemed awfully dangerous, even to me. As I said, in the future I would try this again with far less positive results.

My wheelchair class was one of my favorite classes. I was fortunate to be in the class. I had been begging for more classes and this was one they added to my schedule. Being one of the most disabled people in the class, I was forced to work harder just to keep up.

The rest of the class had Thoracic injuries. A couple of the guys in class became friends of mine. Both individuals were paralyzed because of gunshots to the back. These guys were both in their early twenties and almost seemed proud of their injuries. They indicated to me that their gunshot wounds came as a result of being members in gangs.

I didn't grow up in a rich family, but I was fortunate to grow up in a safe neighborhood where there was no threat of gang violence. My family was much like the family in the TV show "The Walton's". I never argued with my two brothers or two sisters. I remember my father getting angry a few times, and once throwing the Bible across the room, but that was a rare occurrence and he was never physical. We left the doors unlocked and trusted our neighbors.

I was thankful not to have lived in the environment that these two had. They had told me how they grew up around violence. To survive, they became a predator rather than the prey. I can't say I approved of their life choices, but it did give me a different outlook on things. You can't help but wonder what would have happened to these two if they had been raised in my environment, and me in theirs.

I would never steal or hurt another person, but who knows what changes would have occurred if I grew up like they did. They both treated me well and I did not judge them. I also didn't ask them too many questions because I didn't want to judge them.

I was only at RIC for about a week when I heard from Cindy. She and her friend were coming to pick me up in Chicago and take me back to Clinton. The faculty had organized a fund raising event to help earn money for me to help pay medical bills and buy a van with a wheelchair lift. Cindy and her friend came on Friday morning, and once again I wedged my way through the door of the Ford Escort, carefully avoiding getting my Halo bolts caught in the tracks of the chest restraint. It seemed like such a longer trip than what I remembered when I could walk. Unable to re-situate your position was frustrating and uncomfortable.

Miracle recovery takes hard work

■ But Clinton coach is fighting paralysis

By Holly A. Smith
QUAD-CITY TIMES
Clinton bureau

CLINTON, Iowa — David Moore finally can tighten his stomach muscles. Now when he sits up and his body begins to sway to the side, he can pull himself back and straighten his torso.

It's just one of the several miracles Moore, a tennis coach at Clinton High School, has experienced since an Aug. 11 car accident left him paralyzed.

That day, he was on his way home to Clinton from his job at United Parcel Service in Eldridge. He lost control of his car for just a moment, but it was long enough for the car to hit a driveway and flip end-over-end before crashing to the ground.

He broke two vertebrae in his neck and was left without any feeling from the chest down.

Doctors gave him little hope of regaining the use of his limbs.

Since then, he has regained feeling in his arms, thighs and some of his calf muscles.

"Miracles just keep happening for me," he says.

He has built up the strength in his arms so he can maneuver his wheelchair. His days are filled with weight lifting, writing practice and practicing sitting up in bed.

On Friday, he came home for a benefit in his honor. Before the accident, he was the high school's varsity tennis coach and basketball coach at Washington Middle School.

His wife, Cindy Rasche-Moore, teaches music at Washington and also coaches tennis at the high school. Teachers and volunteers planned and orchestrated the benefit supper at Washington.

In the first hour, more than 200 people attended. The minimum donation was $5 and the teachers said many people contributed more. The money will help the Moores purchase a van adapted for him to drive.

The benefit also provided people an opportunity to visit with Moore, who has been in Davenport and Chicago hospitals and

— COACH
Please turn to Page 2A

David Moore, a tennis and basketball coach paralyzed in a car accident, chats with one of his tennis partners, David Brondyke, 9, during a benefit for Moore at Washington Middle School in Clinton, Iowa.
Mark Hagen/QUAD-CITY TIMES

We pulled into the Middle School where Cindy worked as a Music teacher. The fundraiser was held in the cafeteria. The parking lot was already full of cars, but we were able to pull directly up to the front door. Once out of the car and into my chair we headed inside. The ramp leading to the rear doors was too steep for me to climb, and Cindy pushed me into the school. We reached the cafeteria. I rolled through the door and heard a loud applause from the people that came out to see me.

I had always been like my dad. I never saw my dad cry in my entire life, and I never did cry either, but things were different now. I had become a different person. I was someone who could feel joy and pain at a higher level. I felt the pain that others suffered. I appreciated my happiness far more than before. I was fragile, yet stronger than ever. Tears rolled down my cheeks. Feelings overwhelmed me like never before. I ended up in the center of the cafeteria. I sat in my Halo and shook hands with people as they waited their turn in line. Many of the people were friends I hadn't seen since I got into my accident. It was several hours of shaking hands and talking to people.

My injury had left me with some problems with endurance. I'm not sure if it was the shallow breathing or the fact that everything I did took more effort than before, but after a while I was so looking forward to that line ending. I didn't want to appear ungrateful. In fact, I was immensely grateful, but when you start to wear down it's hard to keep pushing forward. I needed this show of support. It renewed my soul, and although physically worn out, it re-energized my spirit. The fundraiser was far more successful than predicted. What a beautiful gesture of support for someone who is struggling. I left the school with a big smile and renewed dedication towards my goals.

I spent that night at home for the first time since my car crash. I was a little afraid of the unknown. Would I have an accident in my sleep? Would I be able to sleep without the attention the nurses offered? Many questions were flashing through my mind, but it all turned out fine.

I saw my daughter on both days. She was one and a half. Maybe it was my Halo or perhaps the fact she hadn't seen me for a while, but she wasn't as enthusiastic as I had hoped. I wanted her to yell "Daddy" and jump into my arms, but she was tentative. She would sit in my lap, but there was a distance that left me feeling sad inside. Just before my accident, we would play. I'd carry her on my shoulders. We'd play hide and seek around cars. We'd sing in the car. I may never be the same dad as I was before. I knew that when I finally returned home, my daughter would love me very much, but it saddened me to think of all those things were going to end.

I needed to return to RIC. It was Sunday, and I had to be back for therapy on Monday. I returned Sunday evening. I had taken my medications while I was gone, and between Cindy's friend, who was a nurse, and Cindy herself, I got catheterized three times each day.

The nurses were ready to start my routine. I eventually moved my bowels and got ready for bed. I had a long week of therapy starting tomorrow.

The beds at RIC had side rails which were great for a person like myself who's arms were getting stronger and stronger, but who couldn't use their lower body. The Halo made movement extremely difficult, but I was able to wedge my arms between the posts of the side rail and pull my body to its' side. I had four pillows in my bed. One was for my head. One was put between my knees, and two were for wedging behind my back. Nurses would get me started for the night. I would wake up numerous times each night, and when I did, I would grab the rails and pull myself from lying on my left side to lying on my back, and later to lying on my right side.

This was one of my first accomplishments, being able to turn myself without the help from the nurses. Placing the pillows behind my back was one of the more difficult things for me to do. I had to wedge my arm between the rails and turn my arm at the elbow in a ninety degree angle, holding me stationary as my body balanced on its' side. My opposite hand would then stuff the pillows behind me. I would then un-wedge my arm, and my body would roll back onto the pillows. I still had people waking me up from time to time, but now I could get a much better night's sleep and it added a bit of independence that I really enjoyed.

I woke up in the morning to Jennifer smiling over my bed. She always had a way of making me feel good. She took my blood pressure, like she always did, and took a sample of blood, which was done periodically. She also catheterized me and helped me get dressed. I was helped into my chair and headed off to breakfast. Transferring from bed to chair was getting progressively easier with each passing day. My physical therapist, Kate, had been working on transfers everyday. I would use the transfer board with Kate and scoot a few inches, move my feet, scoot a few more inches and so on until I was in my chair. The whole time Kate had a good hold onto a gait belt wrapped around my waist and used it to help me keep my balance. I was getting better and better, but my balance was holding me back. I would have liked to try it on my own, but would have probably end up on the floor. I might have had enough strength to pull it off, but my coordination was such that I would most likely fall either forward or backward.

Jennifer normally didn't use a transfer board, but through Kate's urging, Jennifer was working with me much the same way Kate was in therapy.

I rolled to breakfast. It seemed each time I entered the eating area there were a few people missing and a few others that took their place. The turnover rate was a constant thing at RIC. I had excellent insurance through United Parcel Service or I would have been heading home myself, but as I showed improvements the doctors would send out letters to my insurance stressing the importance of staying in rehabilitation. As nice as it would have been to be home, I needed the work the therapists were giving me. They were pushing me and they knew how to give me the opportunity to improve. The work here would dictate how my life would be at home. I wanted to be as healthy and strong as possible when I returned to the "real" world.

I rolled up to one of the dinner tables. An attendant brought me some cereal and then began feeding a young man sitting across from me. He was seventeen years old, and as I would learn from talking to him, was injured when he lost control of his motorcycle. He ran into the front grill of a parked car at about thirty miles per hour. He was thrown head first over the handlebars and slammed his head into the front windshield of the car. The impact broke his neck at C-5. He had some use of his biceps, but no use of his triceps. His hands were nearly useless. The attendant was scooping up his cereal and feeding him. His name was Josh, and there was a quality that I really liked in him. He didn't like needing to be fed, and as the week wore on he began using an attachment to his fingers that would hold his spoon and would try feeding himself. I would sit across from him every day, and watch him make a total mess of himself and the table around him. He would jockey his hand so that his spoon would drop into the cereal bowl, usually with a small splash. Getting the food into the spoon and keeping it there was a real challenge. Once the cereal was in the spoon, it was a long, careful task to get it to the mouth without it tilting and dropping the food all over. Once successfully inserted in the mouth, he used gravity to bring his arm back down.

It's hard to imagine what it's like be without triceps. Triceps do the opposite of biceps. Triceps open the arm and lower the hand. Josh had to figure out how to feed himself with only his biceps. Like myself, he improved every day and sometimes it was just a matter of learning how to do things better.

He was in a power chair that first week, but eventually convinced the therapists to allow him to get a manual wheelchair. His chair had projection rims
like the ones I used at Genesis. Josh's hands and wrists would just hang from
his arms. He found a way to lock them against the vertical projections from
behind him and use his biceps to move a foot or so, then he'd let gravity drop
his arms down and he'd repeat the process. He took forever to get anywhere,
but he hated anyone helping him. I was impressed with his desire and fortitude. The policeman I met when I first arrived had all ready been discharged
and Josh was going to be my new friend.

I grabbed an elevator, which wasn't always easy to do. It all depended
on what floor you were on. RIC is located in a large building. I was never on
every floor, but there were many people working in the building. Elevators
on certain floors, especially in the morning, evening or lunchtime, were very
busy. There were three elevators to the left and three to the right. The doors
would open and it was first come, first serve, as everyone would hurriedly
scurry to the door before the other person. People who can walk have a huge
advantage over those in a wheelchair. If this was a game of musical chairs, I
would definitely have been losing. I would situate myself between two doors
and hope it would be one of those two that opened next. Sometimes I had to
wait a little longer, but eventually I'd catch a door. There were always others
in chairs with the same problem. I wondered if I was like that before my
injury. Would I rush to an elevator door passing by slower people in
wheelchairs? I'm not sure, because I was never in that situation. I don't think
these people were trying to be rude. I think they just weren't being present to
the situation. I've experienced it the other way too! I've been in situations
where other people are ahead of me and they try to put me in front. What I
try to live by is this: if I've waited longer, and I'm ahead, then let me have my
place on the elevator. If not, I'll wait for my turn just like everyone else. I
don't deserve preferential treatment, just equal treatment.

The doors opened to Kate and physical therapy. Kate walked up, and
I followed her into one of the side rooms. Usually our treatment was done in
the main room. In the main room there were numerous mats, each filled
with patients with varying degrees of injury. It always kept me grounded to
see patients who were far worse than myself. Kate took me to a private room
and helped me transfer onto the mat.

After some stretching, she brought out what looked like ropes and pulleys. She fastened velcro cuffs to my ankles and just above the knee. Each cuff had a small hook attached. She arranged her ropes and pulleys from the ceiling and connected them to the cuffs. I would lie on my side as she would adjust the lengths of the rope. My upper leg was suspended in the air horizontally from the ankle and the knee with my leg bent. The leg was about a foot above the mat. From this position, I was able to do some seemingly miraculous things. The knee movement that I had been working on had now become more prominent. I wasn't much stronger, but the elevated leg made the slightest movement much easier. I could straighten my legs out and bring them back in. She had it set up with the knees slightly higher than the ankles. This made it slightly harder to straighten my leg than to close it. She did this because my quadriceps were stronger than my hamstrings. I could work my legs for a long time in this position. My movements were much more pronounced, and because it took less effort, my endurance was greatly increased.

My workouts were much more like I remembered from before the accident. Working my legs up until now was just to make them move a few times and then rest until I could try again. Now I could keep them moving for minutes without a break and the fact that I could move them much further gave me the illusion of improvement that I needed to push me forward. I was just beginning my renaissance of treatment. During the renaissance there was an explosion of creativity and discovery and my micro renaissance started the day I was connected to those ropes and had my first workout. Kate would turn me to the other side and have me work the other leg before treatment ended.

I left what I would always call "Rope Therapy," and headed over to see my occupational therapist, Melissa. Melissa also had a treat for me. She had the Stander all set up and ready for me. The Stander is a device with all kinds of straps and supports so that when you're properly adjusted, it can hoist you up and keep you in a standing position whether you have any strength in your lower body or not. It relies on locking your legs at the knee and at the hips, and supporting the rest of your body.

A stander should be something every person who can't stand should own or at least have access to use.

Unfortunately, most insurance companies don't necessarily agree with me, at least with the owning part. A Stander does so many positive things for the body. It increases blood pressure. Dizziness and passing out happens often to people with spinal cord injury. After injury, the blood pressure drops drastically and it has potentially more negative effects than just causing a person to become lightheaded. Low blood pressure also increases your chances for blood clots, among other things, and blood clots can be deadly.

Standing also increases bone density. Over time, most spinal cord injured people end up with frail bones that can break easily. Early on, when the nurses first starting using a catheter, I found myself experiencing considerable pain. I thought I wasn't supposed to feel pain, because I couldn't feel pain on the surface, but I could feel it internally. My initial inactivity caused my bones to break down. Calcium from my bones formed small granular pellets the size of rice. These pellets would eventually be expelled through my bladder. I'm sure that anyone who has experienced stones can tell you, it doesn't feel good, and for me it indicated my bone density had diminished. This was bone that was breaking down and being discarded by my body.

The Stander offers so many benefits it amazes me they're not used more than they are. I am happy to say Melissa would put me in a Stander on a regular basis, and many times for the entire hour. She wouldn't stop at just that. She would bring me hand exercises and even play games that required me to handle cards and such while I stood in the Stander, just to make the most of my hour.

I can't tell you how incredibly awesome it feels to be in a standing position after being in a wheelchair for the past few months. I forgot how tall I was. I was finally looking down at all the things I had been looking up at. It helped so much with my psyche. Recovering from accidents like this are more than just about the physical, it's also about the mental. From experience, I believe it's even more about the mental. It's the mental thoughts that push the physical actions. It's the mental that controls the cells in your body and encourages healing. It's the mental that pushes you when you're tired and want to stop. Anytime I could feel myself improving, whether real or just a machine like a Stander, it made me feel as though I was healing. This feeling revitalized my dream of beating this and returning to the place I was before I drove off that road; the time when everything was easy, and unfortunately, sometimes taken for granted.

My sleeping at night was becoming more difficult, but that was okay. I would lay in bed and feel my body burn. I pondered if this might be a similar feeling women go through during menopause. I spent much of my time trying to understand and figure things out, but rarely with success. After exhausting all my strength for the day I'd retire to bed. I always felt my body parts burning, burning much like my quadriceps had done earlier. A hot like sensation that is hard to describe, but is what I imagined a swarm of bees all stinging me at once might feel like. It made it hard to sleep but that was fine with me. I would close my eyes and imagine the burning part as being healed. I would think of small cells and nerves all coming together to connect and work as one. I imagined my neck at the site of the injury freeing up a channel and nerves running through and down my body. I always went from body part to body part trying to move anything I could.

I found with time that areas that were burning were signs that that area was trying to heal. I envisioned the nerves snapping off in succession as they tried to re-ignite. It was never explained what was going on, but I knew it was a sign that I needed to work those specific areas. I relayed this thought to Kate, my physical therapist. I think she was a bit skeptical at first, but I told her how my ankles were burning, and sure enough, my ankles eventually started moving. Kate ultimately came on board. I would arrive at therapy and if I had any new burning sensations she would include them in our workouts. We would spend two to three hours a day doing "Rope Therapy". My body wasn't re-awakening quickly, but it was steady. When an area would start burning, it would burn night after night and during the day. It might take weeks before I could move that body part, but in time I always did.

I had thought recovery would come all at once. That I would somehow use my inner prayers and focus to heal my neck, movement, and the ability to feel would cascade down my neck and through my body. I would then just stand up and walk out; but it didn't work that way. It was long, it was hard, and it was slow going. It was piece by piece and not the body as a whole. It also wasn't complete. I was regaining the ability to move body parts, but the strength was far less than before and the control was, well, pathetic. When I say control, I'm referring to the ability to stop your body at a certain point, to move it at a certain speed, and being able to move it in any direction.

Major muscles were returning, but it was a matter of me concentrating, and then, with effort, contracting that muscle. Wherever it moved to, it moved to.

I also want to mention very emphatically that this was by no means a purely physical accomplishment. I was in the process of training my brain through constant trial and error. It is so hard to describe to someone that has always been able bodied, but I will do my best. What I'm about to say is what I learned through my own experiences. I'm not even sure the medical field would agree or understand, but from what I've learned, all I can say is that I am absolutely convinced.

I was able to move various body parts by thinking differently about how to move them. My theory is that from conception we have trained our brains on how we must think to move an arm or a leg, etc. With each thought, a nerve follows a path down the spinal cord to that area and con-tracts the proper muscles to make your thought a reality. After we think the same way for a long enough time, the need for thought becomes less and less until finally it becomes nearly automatic. An able bodied person walks and moves almost as if no thought process was needed. To move an arm we just move it. The thought is so easy it is sometimes overlooked.

After my injury, if I tried to move anything below my injury line, nothing would happen. Even after the burning sensations I described earlier, thinking the same way as I always had wouldn't work. The paths that had previously allowed my nerves to travel were now blocked through damage and scar tissue. However, because my injury was incomplete, parts of my spinal cord was still intact and some paths were still open. I needed to begin thinking differently. I needed to send my nerves down the paths that were still open and have them reach their intended target.

I would lay in bed (and I did this throughout the day as well), and concentrate on the part of the body I wanted to move. It is imperative to continue concentrating on the area that you want to move. The nerves need to know their destination. Then, and it's so hard to explain, you need to keep your mind open to trying new ways to think of moving that part. Don't keep thinking the same way when you don't receive results, because you'll continue to obtain those same results. I would concentrate on a particular body part or muscle and then vary my thoughts on how to move that area while envisioning my nerves searching out and finding new paths.

It had been months now of meditating on healing, and like everything else, you improve with practice. My injury and isolation left me with little outside distraction and I was able to focus much better than those early days in the hospital. I think of the abilities of the Tibetan monks living their whole life without distractions and spending much of their life in meditation. I saw a documentary once where monks were given a wet towel to wrap around their shirtless upper body and put inside a refrigerated room. Most people would have suffered hypothermia, but the monks, through meditation, were able to warm their bodies to the point you could see steam coming off the wet towels. The body is an amazing thing. The body is constantly trying to heal itself. I knew my body wanted to heal itself, but for whatever reason, it doesn't know how to heal the spinal cord. I've heard scientists say it's because in the wild, an animal or person suffering a spinal cord injury would surely die. Thereby, evolution never had a chance of adapting to such injuries But these same people also said the brain couldn't repair itself, and we have since learned it can, even if such repair is seemingly limited.

My meditation allowed my nerves to follow new paths to reach their desired destinations. Many of my nerves were destroyed when my spinal cord was swollen, and many of the paths in my cord were damaged as well. Fewer paths with fewer nerves means a limited recovery, but I still can't give up on the ability of the human body to find a way to make up for this limitation. This is what I believe. This is what I've learned through experiencing it.

Although weak, I can move my arms in the same way as I always did. My hands and triceps are affected, but when I want my arms to move, they do with little thought. I'm assuming my spinal cord was only temporarily shocked in those areas, but it makes me think why my arms were affected at all. Why were they so weak for so long, only to continue to get stronger with time? The mysteries of the spinal cord are many. My hope is that they'll uncover those mysteries and solve the problems so many people must face with spinal cord injury.

CHAPTER NINE
My New Roommates

It was just after dinner when they brought in Timothy. I was lying in bed when the ruckus began. A male nurse and two attendants were wheeling a patient into my room. They wheeled his stretcher alongside the bed that was vacant in the opposite corner from mine.

It was obvious this man was in bad shape. His eyes were closed and there was a gurgling sound coming from his throat. His hands were laid out across his body much like you see with a corpse when you attend a visitation. He was motionless. I wasn't sure if he was conscious or not, but the three men were busy preparing to move him onto the bed. The gurgling sound was intermittent, and it seemed like breathing. The three men tilted him to the side and slid a board beneath his body. Then they lifted the board and moved him to the bed, tilted his body, and slid the board out from under him. I was lying on my side watching the whole scenario unfold. A female nurse entered the room and suctioned out the tracheal tube that was causing that horrible gurgling sound. The gurgling stopped and the nurses continued attending to him the best they could for the next thirty minutes or so. The gurgling would return after a short time and the day nurses were constantly coming in to suction out his tube. I would come to find out that he had spent the past few weeks in Intensive Care battling pneumonia. He was now cleared for admission into RIC.

I was surprised he was here. He was stick thin, had light sandy brown hair and looked tall, probably six foot five. He struggled breathing and looked like he should be under constant care. The gurgling sound would return after a half hour or so and just kept getting worse until cleared out.

I couldn't help but think how lucky I was. I was never as bad as this. I was never battling for my life. If he had improved so much, how bad was he before?

I had closed my eyes. My sleeping was still more a collection of naps than a good nights sleep. My sleep was light and any sound or disturbance would wake me. I heard the voices of children as I opened my eyes and I saw Timothy, or Tim, as I would come to know him. Tim had seven children surrounding his bed in ages from two to twelve, and accompanied by a woman who appeared to be their mother. I assumed that this was his wife and kids. There was no exchange between Tim and his family. It was clear the family was very concerned about his condition. The only sound I heard was hushed questions from the kids to their mother, most of which were questions about their father's health. It was a sad and surreal scene. It makes a person, even a person like myself, appreciate their health.

My nightly meditation would always include Tim. I couldn't bring myself to pray for my own recovery before his. I prayed for Tim's recovery, even if recovery only meant getting healthy enough to talk to his kids. It reminded me of those first few days after my accident. How fragile life is. I grew up thinking I was invincible, but how deluded my thinking was. There's a fine line between life and death, health and sickness. When you realize this, you tend to appreciate life all the more when you do have your health.

I woke up in the middle of the night to that same gurgling sound. I expected a nurse to enter the room at any time to suction out his air hole and give him some needed relief, but it never came. The gurgling just kept getting worse, and I could see him straining to breathe. He was thrashing his head from side to side and that sound of someone struggling for every breath haunted me to my core. I began yelling for someone to help, but my voice was still hollow and soft. No one would hear me unless they were very close.

I was aware of the emergency button located over every bed. It was placed high above the bed for the staff to use and not necessarily the patients. I've read about people who are capable of amazing feats when encountering an emergency situation. I locked my arm around the headboard and yanked myself as high as I could, then reached with my off hand as far as I possibly could. I wasn't quite there and pulled myself a few inches higher and hit the button.

Red lights started flashing and an alarm was set off. In moments, there were numerous people in the room and they immediately began working on Tim. It was such a relief to hear the gurgling stop and his breathing become regular. I heard them questioning each other and asking who had hit the emergency button. Eventually they worked their way over to my bed and I told them that I had been the one that set off the alarm. They couldn't quite figure out how I was able to do it, and frankly, I still don't know how I did it. Perhaps a prayer was answered! I told the people around my bed that he needed to be checked on regularly. I remember one of the men coming up to me and thanking me. I really appreciated him doing that. Many of the least-best workers did the night shift. It was obvious the day shift was far more vigilant than the night shift. I had trouble sleeping the rest of that night. I felt like I was Tim's protector. We had both suffered similar situations, and it was up to me to make sure he got the care he needed.

I awoke to Jennifer looking over my bed. She had a big grin on her face and said she was late because she had come from a special meeting. She said the meeting was about the alarm that was set off that evening. She said she heard I was the one that set it off. I replied "yes". She said those alarms are very important and should only be used in emergencies. She told me they discussed Tim's situation and the need for him to be under constant observation. They discussed the possibility of Tim drowning, and how it may have happened that night had the alarm not been set off. Jennifer, with her big grin and piercing brown eyes told me "Thank you" as well.

There was a connection from that moment on that was very special. She became more than a nurse, but a very good friend. You sometimes meet people in your life and you feel a connection; an understanding. You understand what they're thinking and you feel comfortable. I felt that with Jennifer. Jennifer and her fiancé would take me out to dinner before I got discharged. She would invite me to her wedding in a few years and even have a special dance with me in front of her guests. I think of Jennifer and I think of a beautiful, caring, loving person whom I will always cherish.

This had been Tim's first night at RIC. I never mentioned what had happened that night. I'm not sure the staff described it to him either. I don't believe he was fully present due to the Morphine drip he was connected to.

The next few days would see Tim get stronger and stronger and need less pain medications.

It was another typical day of sitting down with Josh. Josh was the young kid who had the motorcycle accident. His improvements were small but noticeable. There seemed to be less of a mess each day at the table and he always kept me smiling. It might seem strange to some people, but we were always laughing with, and at, each other. We were living with our problems each day and there is only so much grief a person can feel before it starts dragging you down. There comes a point when you have to accept the situation you're in and find the humor in it. We weren't accepting that we were going to stay in our present condition, but laughing each day at our limitations was a far healthier way of spending our time than having the attitude of feeling sorry for yourself. New people were being admitted nearly every day. It's amazing how many people suffer catastrophic accidents in this world.

A young girl named Shelley joined our table that morning. Shelley had been admitted the previous night at the same time as Tim. Shelley was in her late teens and had been in an automobile accident like myself. She had fire red hair that was thick and full of curls. She had bright red freckles covering her cute round face. She had a light complexion and was very petite. I'm sure she weighed under a hundred pounds. Her injury appeared to be similar to Josh. She was a fighter, but chose to use a power chair, which was a good choice in her situation. She had trouble moving her arms and I think pushing her own chair would have been a stretch. Shelley's power chair had a small toggle that operated the chair. It rotated in all directions and she seemed to have had some experience with it. She mentioned that another girl was admitted in her room last night as well. Her name was Karen, and she sat at the table across from ours.

Karen was also in her teens, but quite different than Shelley. Karen was tall, thin, with long legs. She looked like a girl you'd expect to be playing volleyball or basketball. She had blonde hair that was straight and flowed down to the middle of her back. Karen had large blue eyes, and a small mouth. She had her family with her and a young man about her age. It seemed likely the young man was her boyfriend and not her brother by the way he cared for her. He would scoop up cereal into the spoon and gently hold it to her mouth until she swallowed.

Her mother was by her side looking for ways to help, but at the moment there really wasn't any more that could be done. Karen also had a power wheelchair, and like Josh and Shelley, she appeared to have broken her neck at about C-5. She could move her arms with effort, but she had major difficulties with her hands, wrists, and triceps.

I was at a point now that I could make an educated guess as to the level of a person's injury just by what that person could and could not do. The injury level at each cervical vertebra makes such a huge difference in what the body is capable of doing. Had my injury been one vertebra lower I would have full function of my hands, but one vertebra higher and I may not be able to use my triceps. At vertebrae C-5, one higher may mean a loss of your arms altogether. I looked around at all the patients in the room that were moving their chairs by blowing into a straw, whose arms and hands were uselessly laid out onto their arm rests. Hands straight down with all five fingers laid flat. They would move these titanic sized tanks by blowing into a small straw that hung precipitously close to their lips. When you see the struggles these people have, I cannot possibly imagine ever feeling sorry for myself.

That day in therapy I had been having burning sensations in my hip, so Kate had me strung up on my back with my knee extended above my body with ropes. I wasn't able to move my hips, but I focused on them whenever I had a chance. I should have embraced occupational therapy more. I did try my best, but some of the things we did would frustrate me greatly. Melissa would place small objects in front of me and have me try and pick them up, like paper clips or coins. I remember getting so flustered at failure after failure that it drove me crazy. Such a simple task that was never a problem in the past was now such a major endeavor.

One thing you must learn when you become a spinal cord injured person is patience. Everything takes longer and some things are much harder to do. There are many tasks that are seemingly impossible to do. I think when you are freshly injured, it's even more frustrating because you still remember so vividly what it was like before when you could spring up from the couch and pour a bowl of cereal or pick up a coin and drop it into a vending machine. I could do those same tasks, but now it took much longer. I may have failed time after time, but eventually I got that coin in my hand and inserted it in the machine without dropping it first.

When I did drop it, how agonizingly long it took before I could pick it up again. I must be aware of being patient. Realizing that things will take time, and that tasks will be difficult, but that perseverance is the key and a positive attitude a must.

I finished my day of classes and went to dinner. I sat with the two young patients Josh and Shelley. I also sat with Matt. This was one of the few nights I had gotten a chance to speak with Matt. He was seldom without his mother when he wasn't in therapy. Matt was getting discharged on Friday, which was only three days from now. Matt was a very nice young man. His arms were very weak like Josh's, but he was able to move them. He was in a manual wheelchair, but almost always had someone pushing him from place to place. It seemed he had been sheltered most of his life, and now with his paralysis, sheltered even more. I'm not here to judge, but through my eyes he was being held back. His life was very comfortable and he was loved deeply, but he had gotten to the point that he didn't even bother to do things on his own anymore. It felt as though a spirit within him was diminished, and his lust for life somewhat muted.

Josh and I were signed up for an RIC outing the following day. RIC offered special outings every couple of weeks, and tomorrow we were going bowling. We were able to talk Matt and Shelley into joining us the following evening.

The next night we gathered for our bowling trip. There were about ten people signed up for the trip and we ended up taking two of the RIC vans. They each had lifts for the wheelchairs, and workers from RIC would take us up one by one and once inside, strap our chairs down. Besides Josh, Matt, and Shelley, Karen had also joined us. She had heard about the trip from Shelley. This was my first time sitting in a wheelchair aboard a moving vehicle. Each time the van would accelerate, decelerate, or take a turn, the wheelchair would lurch in that direction only to be caught by the straps holding it in place. It felt as though you would fly across the vehicle at any time, but the van was well equipped and the chair was secure. It was dark as I stared out the window. Chicago is a big place. I had no idea where we were, but in about fifteen minutes we had arrived at the bowling alley.

The trip was fun for the fact that I got to know Matt and Karen better. Matt was excited to finally be leaving and heading home. He was going to live with his mom and she had all ready made many accommodations to the house. She had a roll-in shower installed. She had a ramp built leading up to the front door. She had grab bars put in. RIC has personnel that will go to a person's house and make recommendations to make it suitable for the patients, and Matt's mother had taken their advice. Matt lived in Chicago and had been home most weekends, but Friday he was going home for good. It crossed my mind that staying a little longer might be good for him, but he was anxious to be getting home and I was happy for him.

Karen lived a few hours away. Karen was a very sweet young girl and as I suspected, was with her boyfriend the previous day. She was actually engaged. She was twenty years old. I was absolutely stunned when she told me how she got injured. She hadn't been in a car accident or even a motorcycle accident. She was visiting her mother when it happened. She was standing in a hallway talking with her mother. She took a step back, lost her balance and fell over backward. She said that as she fell her head hit the wall behind her. She crumbled to the ground and couldn't move. The mother called an ambulance. She found out later she had broken her neck at C-5.

It was hard for me to believe. I wondered how incredibly unlucky this poor girl was. How many times have we all fallen only to get up, brush off the dirt, and go on our merry way, never to think anymore about it? I didn't know such a freak accident was even possible. The wall must have been just the perfect distance away and she must have hit it just right. Without sound-ing redundant, it's amazing how quickly a life can change.

We all bowled a couple of games before heading back. They had ramps set up that faced the pins. We would tell the attendants which direction we wanted the ramps to face. The attendant would place the ball on top of the ramp and let us hold it in place. We then let go of the bowling ball. The ball rolled down the ramp and onto the lane and hopefully hit some pins. They even had those plastic rolls in the gutter so the ball would just ricochet back onto the lane if it headed that way. The bowling part was kind of boring. I enjoyed getting out of RIC and getting a chance to know Matt and Karen better, but for me this wasn't really bowling.

It was late when we arrived back at the center and the night nurse was anxious to dispense medications. They liked to give medications early. They had a cart full of medications and would go from door to door filling up little paper cups with the patient's pills. There were three or four for me each night, and I had missed her as she made her rounds. I rolled into the room with her right behind me. I took my pills and noticed I had two new roommates. I now had three roommates and the room was full. Everyone was sleeping and Tim's gurgling had improved greatly.

I awoke the next morning to many voices. My curtains were pulled so I couldn't tell what was going on, but I could hear Jennifer's voice and Dr. Wang's as well. They were going from bed to bed talking to the patients and taking care of their needs. I was the last one. My curtains were opened and I could see the empty beds. The other patients had already been put into wheelchairs and taken out. I told Dr. Wang that I was fine, just as my legs flew into the air with a spasm. He asked me again to take spasm medication and I agreed. I'm not sure why I agreed at that moment. He must have caught me at just the right time. Again, I took them for just a week or so and then asked to be taken off them. My spasms didn't hurt, but as I learned from Tim that isn't always the case. I would hear Tim groan from across the room as he endured spasms. It was just one more thing for me to be grateful for.

That evening after therapy and dinner I stayed up to watch a movie. Periodically RIC would have movies in a side room just off the area where we ate. RIC always had plenty of volunteers that enjoyed coming in and helping make our lives a little better. I forget what movie was playing, but I do remember the popcorn. The volunteers had made bags of popcorn and handed them out to everyone who wanted them. It had been a long time since I had popcorn. Sadly it was only salted, and was completely absent of the butter I usually soaked my popcorn in. I remember eating the popcorn, one popped piece at a time. I had always eaten my popcorn by the handfuls but my hands wouldn't allow it. I was hungry and forced to sustain my hunger one measly piece at a time. I tried! Believe me, I tried to grab a handful and get that handful to my mouth, but each time I ended up with an empty palm to my lips and a pile of popcorn on my lap and floor.

I eventually resigned myself to the fact I was going to eat this bag of popcorn one kernel at a time, and that's exactly what I did. I probably don't remember the movie because I spent the whole time trying to get that next piece of popcorn to my mouth. My occupational therapist Melissa would have been very proud of me that night. After the movie, I rolled back to my room.

I entered the room and Tim's family was just saying their goodbyes. The other two roommates were awake as well. I stopped and talked to Tim before the night nurse arrived to get me ready for bed. Tim was a farmer who lived in Indiana. He was also a huge Purdue fan. He was surprisingly cheerful for a man who could only move from the neck up. I asked him what had happened and he proceeded to tell me. He had been working on a ladder up on the side of a silo when the step he was standing on broke causing him to fall backward thirty feet. He had hit the ground head first. One of his kids witnessed what had happened, and ran to tell his wife who called an ambulance. He had injured both C-3 and C-4. He was paralyzed from the neck down. His breathing was strained, but he could still breathe. He was taken to the hospital where they confirmed he had a complete injury. A complete injury is slang meaning the spinal cord was completely severed. When the cord is severed there is little to no chance of regaining any movement.

I have learned over time that many "complete injuries" aren't necessarily complete at all. It is very difficult to completely sever the spinal cord. Perhaps a bullet would, but not usually a situation where bone fragments enter into the cord. Nonetheless, his injury was very severe and his prognosis was not good. Even if his cord didn't improve, Tim had a long way to go to improve his health. He looked beaten and tired, which made his smile all the more befuddling. I thought of myself as strong, but Tim was stronger than me. I wondered if I could handle what he's gone through. I have had able-bodied people say to me. "I could never handle your situation as well as you", but until you're put into that situation you never really know. When put in tough situations, we are capable of doing things that far surpasses what we believe we're capable of. Perhaps I could handle Tim's fate, but I'm thankful I don't have to find out. I said hi to the other two roommates as the night nurse rolled me to my bed and closed the curtains.

She administered a suppository and transferred me onto a shower chair. A shower chair has a metal frame with a plastic doughnut seat on top. The opening in the seat resembles that of a toilet. Underneath the seat the nurse would place a bucket with a plastic liner. I hate "Digistim," as I think most people would. I would insist on the nurses and staff allowing me time to let the suppository do its' work and see if I could move my bowels without the use of Digistim. Sometimes I was lucky and could bypass this invasive procedure, while other times, not so much.

Everyone else had all ready been taken care of, but since I was late from my movie, they still had to take care of me. After a half hour on the shower chair I had some luck. I found resting my chest against my knees and pulling my knees in as tight as possible while still wearing a Halo and vest would sometimes get the whole process going. That night I avoided Digistim and got to sleep. I wouldn't have to worry about all this for two more nights.

The next morning at breakfast I got the opportunity to talk briefly with my two new roommates. Their names were John and Roger. Roger was in his forties and looked healthy and fit. He was better off than the vast majority of the patients here. He was about five foot ten and weighed one sixty. He had a long nose and rugged facial features. His reddish blonde hair was receding at the brow. Roger had broken his lower back and was in a Tortoise shell. He got around well and could easily use his arms to transfer from chair to seat.

Roger was injured while jumping out of a plane. He jumped from a plane with an automatic parachute on his back. This is a chute that doesn't require you to pull a cord. The chute will automatically open on it's own. He told me he was supposed to count to ten, and if for some reason the parachute fails to open, he should then pull the cord to the back up chute and float safely down. He jumped from the plane and forgot to count. He then panicked, and pulled his back up chute just as his regular chute opened. The two chutes became tangled and he fell at a much quicker rate than was safe. He hit the ground hard breaking his lower back.

John was an older man in his early sixties. He had thinning brown hair and could move one wrist. He couldn't move either arm but being able to move that one wrist allowed John to use a power chair.

The way he would throw his hand against the control knob was a bit erratic. He often hit the walls when taking corners and I wouldn't want to be walking too close to him when he was driving. John liked to keep to himself, and it would take awhile for me to get to know him. Roger, the parachutist, on the other hand was a person who was always talking. I think he liked to hear himself talk. He was the guy who waited for you to quit talking so he could resume his own conversation. A man who always knew more than anyone else, and made sure everyone knew it. It might be unkind to describe him this way, but I'm being as accurate as I can be. I never really developed a close relationship with Roger. The fact is, I usually avoided him. I liked to keep positive energy running through and around me, and Roger always seemed to make that difficult.

That Friday morning at breakfast, we all said our goodbyes to Matt. His mother was there, and everyone wore a smile. The nurses and attendants were there as well. I imagined it being similar to an inmate on his day of release. He was leaving, but we were still serving our sentence. I really hoped everything would work out for Matt and wished him the very best for the future. I watched as his mother wheeled him out the door.

CHAPTER TEN
Heading to the Doctor

I had a couple of appointments set up for me in the next few days. I had seen the doctor on his regular visits, and had had some urinary tract infections. As I mentioned before, anyone sending a catheter from the unsanitary outside world into your sanitary bladder is at a risk of contracting infection. The nurse would take urine samples and have them tested periodically for infection. If they found an infection, the lab would then test the infection against various antibiotics to determine which would work best. I had two infections until now, and nearly everyone else had similar experiences. We would be prescribed Penicillin or Amoxicillin or one of many other "Cillins" out there. We'd take the pills for ten days, and usually the problem would be solved.

My first appointment was to see a urological specialist. I wasn't completely sure why I had to see this doctor, but it was on my schedule and it meant missing a couple hours of therapy to attend. I wasn't allowed to just wheel my chair to the proper floor. Instead, my nurse Jennifer dressed me in a hospital gown and I was wheeled in a gurney to the doctor's office. I was in the hallway a long time. I wondered if they had forgotten about me, but after about thirty minutes they rolled me into what looked like an operating room. The doctor and his staff inserted a special catheter that was connected to a machine. Sensors were placed around my lower abdomen and the doctor began pumping fluid into my bladder. The doctor asked me to tell him if I felt the "urge to pee". I waited, but felt nothing. I could hear the machine working and I knew it was filling up my bladder. I wanted to feel something. I closed my eyes and so wanted to feel something.

I'm still not sure if I really felt the urge to pee or not, but I do know that I convinced myself that I did. I said "I feel it," and he measured the amount of fluid he had pumped into my bladder and checked for any contractions or movements within the bladder. He then continued to put more fluid inside of me. I felt confident I could feel the need to go to the bathroom, but it wasn't obvious and it might have been just wishful thinking on my part. When he had finished taking his tests he drained my bladder and sent me on my way. Before I left the room, he told me that my body was still healing, and that I was going to keep improving. I wondered at the time, how he could say such a thing to me? Up until now, every doctor made a conscious effort to downplay my recovery. To give me as little hope as possible so that I wouldn't have false expectations. But this doctor broke the mold and was going out on a limb, telling me I was going to improve. I wondered what he saw that all these other doctors missed. I had all ready discarded all the other doctor's words of gloom, and it was refreshing to hear a doctor say what I had been hoping to hear, that my body wasn't at a standstill. I was going to continue to improve, but that's what I believed deep in my heart from the beginning anyway.

That evening I was talking to John. John was from Chicago. When he described his life before the accident, it became clear that John was used to the finer things. Money did not seem to be a problem in John's life. John's voice was strong for his injury. He was able to avoid pneumonia in those early stages and it allowed his body to heal much more quickly. He had use of his wrist and that enabled him to drive his power chair. Perhaps wildly, but drive it nonetheless.

John eventually mentioned the day he suffered his injury. He was open and candid with what happened, which seemed typical of most people suffering from a life altering injury. Telling miss truths or white lies doesn't seem necessary. So much is taken away; and you are left with just those things you find truly important, like the people around you. There is no need to represent yourself in a false light. Truth is the only option. A life altering injury allows you to find the person you really are, which so many times are disguised by all our desires; to be something or someone else.

John was attending a party of a friend. He was married, but his wife was not with him at the party.

His secretary was, however, and it was this secretary that he was having an affair with. He was standing outside by the pool talking to a group of colleagues, a martini in his hand. John had somehow slipped and fell backward into the shallow end of the pool. John paused and his voice lowered as if about to tell a secret. He said "I have always been the type of person who didn't believe in God, didn't believe in spirits or an afterlife. I believed that people who believed in such things were nuts. I was sure there was nothing after you died but an eternal sleep, but I promise you what I'm about to say really happened. I'm not making it up." He looked at me like he thought I was going to get a straight jacket right then and there and wrap him up in it. The look in his face was like someone who questioned their own sanity, and a look of desperation pleading for me not to question it as well.

"I felt myself leave my body and float up over the pool," John said "I was looking down at my body. It was lying underneath the water. I saw my body on the floor of the pool. There were people from the party looking down at my body. A couple of men jumped in and pulled me out of the water and began trying to resuscitate me. It was so clear! I recognized all the people that were there. I was actually watching my rescue take place in front of my eyes and it wasn't a vision. I saw it, and I never would have believed it, but there is something after death, I'm sure of it. I then felt myself slowly descending towards my body and the next thing I remember was waking up in the hospital and them telling me I had nearly died."

I was always open-minded to the thought of your soul rising up out of your body after death. I had heard of many similar stories, but never knew the people or what their beliefs were. John's experience held extra weight with me. I knew he hadn't believed in this sort of thing beforehand, and I could see the difficulty he had in telling me this, but yet somehow felt the need to. Through this accident, John's wife found out about his affair and divorced him. His secretary showed up a few times at the hospital, but soon, I never saw her again either. It seemed John had lost a bit more from this injury than just his health.

A few days later I found myself again heading to see a doctor, but for a completely different reason. The moment I had been waiting months for had finally arrived. I was scheduled to get my Halo removed. I had seen other patients get their Halos removed.

Matt, the young man who had been discharged a week earlier with his mom was one, and what a difference. You get so accustomed to seeing a person through bars that when the Halo comes off, it's like looking at a totally different person. Matt had told me that after his Halo was removed he had trouble holding his head up. His neck muscles had atrophied. He wore a neck brace for numerous days afterwards until his neck muscles became stronger.

I was allowed to roll my chair to the doctor's office, which is located within the RIC building. I had hoped he was just going to take a screwdriver and undo the brace from my head, pop off the vest and I'd be on my way, but first he had to take some x-rays. He needed to make sure the fused area of my neck had fully healed from my accident. This was the first time anyone had taken a look at my injured area since my bones were fused. If my bones didn't look right, I wouldn't be getting the Halo off that day. Once the x-rays were taken I waited in an adjacent room. I waited until the doctor returned with the images of my spine. This was the first time I had a chance to see my damaged spine. I could easily see where the bones were fused. I could see each independent vertebrae starting at the top of the neck and then the last three looked like one long bone stretching to my shoulders.

This doctor was considered one of the best doctors in his field, and he was very impressed with the job my original physician had done back in Davenport, Iowa. He had taken bone from my left hip and fashioned vertebrae to replace my shattered ones. The RIC doctor said he had done a great job, and the bones had healed well. In just a few minutes he had the vest off and was unscrewing the bolts from my skull. The nurse supported my neck as he removed the Halo. It didn't hurt a bit.

What a strange sensation to have my neck supporting my head again. The doctor asked me to move my neck from side to side and up and down in a slow and controlled manner. I had lost quite a bit of mobility. I couldn't turn my neck completely to the side and I couldn't look completely up or down. He gave me some exercises to do with my neck to increase its' mobility. My head felt heavy, but my neck was strong enough to support it. I believe my neck was still strong because of all the exertion in therapy, and especially the weightlifting class I took each day. These were the activities that when I strained I could sometimes hear my Halo creak. Whenever I strained to lift or move I would tense up my neck and put stress on my Halo.

This loosened the Halo, but it also kept my neck somewhat strong, at least stronger than it would have been otherwise. I was able to leave the doctors office without wearing a neck brace.

Rolling my chair down the hallway was such a strange feeling. I had gotten so accustomed to this bulky thing restricting my movement. Although my neck was somewhat strong, I was conscious of using it to hold my head up. When wearing the Halo I had to turn my entire upper body to see around me, but now I could just turn my head. I took my hand and rolled it over the top of my head. It was something I hadn't been able to do for months.

It was late in the day and I was already a little late for dinner. As I rolled into the eating area, patients and nurses were surprised to see my face without looking through steel girders. It would only take a couple of days before it all seemed normal again. My neck would be strong and I would realize that I was capable of doing quite a bit more in therapy without that confining Halo and vest limiting me.

Tracy came by my room that evening. Tracy was the first therapist I met when I arrived here at RIC. She was the beautiful girl who had given me my first shower. Tracy was always a happy girl with a big smile. She seemed truly excited to see me without my Halo. She helped me transfer into the bed and pulled my curtains. She helped me get undressed and into a night gown and then she helped transfer me into a shower chair. She wheeled me across the hall and to the shower.

The feeling in my body had been slowly improving since I had been there, and when Tracy turned the water on, I felt it hit my skin. I could actually feel it. It wasn't like before my injury, but I could feel it. I couldn't feel hot or cold below my injury line, but I could feel the pressure of the spray as it struck my skin. The feeling was muted. The best way I can describe it is that it felt as though I was wearing tight, thin leather clothes over my body. The intense sensitive sensation on my outer skin was absent, but my body's ability to feel pressure was intact. I would find out in time that my ability to feel pain on my outer skin was absent as well. I could feel inner pain, but the surface of my skin couldn't feel pain at all. You could take a razor blade and cut me and it wouldn't hurt, but I might be able to feel the pressure of the blade if you pressed hard enough.

Tracy wore plastic gloves and used a large sponge and washcloth. The shower had a mobile spray head that she held in her hand as she soaped up my body and sprayed me clean. She began by washing my hair. It was such a treat to have my scalp massaged. I think Tracy realized how much I enjoyed it, because she massaged the shampoo into my hair for a very long time. She washed my chest, and though I had my chest washed before, it still felt incredibly good after wearing that wool lined vest.

Tracy was in front of me with her knees bent in a squatting position rinsing down my chest and abdomen, sprayer in hand. She told me she was going to wash between my legs, which meant she was going to wash my genitals. I guess she wanted to prepare me, but when you've been in the kind of situation I had been in the past few months, all shyness is gone. I'm sure it's similar to a woman giving childbirth. There comes a time when you don't think of the body in a sexual way anymore. It just becomes another part of your body. I can't help but think what a healthier world we would have if we all thought that way all the time. A world where there weren't hang-ups, or obsessions with the human body. Where we viewed the human body as a beautiful thing.

Tracy began soaping down my genitals and then, still in a squatting position, she leaned in with her washcloth and began washing underneath my Scrotum. The moment that washcloth touched my Perineum, or in slang, the choad (the area that is between your scrotum and your anus), I felt my legs go into a massive spasm. Tracy was leaning in with her washcloth and her head was between my legs as my spasm kicked into full force. My knees flew together catching both sides of Tracy's forehead and holding her tight. Tracy, sprayer in one hand, washcloth in the other, was desperately flailing her head. She was using her legs to help pull back, but the strength of the spasm was intense and her head stayed locked between my knees. There was nothing I could do either, but just wait for the spasm to subside. When the spasm finally ended she yanked her head out from between my knees and stood up. She looked at me with a monstrous grin and laughingly said with a bright red face, "Don't you dare tell a single person about what just happened". Of course, I told about anyone who would take the time to listen. I learned over time, that this area of my body always seemed to trigger a spasm.

Sometimes just pulling on underwear would cause my legs to lock together. Every time I'd see Tracy she'd give me that cheshire grin of hers, and I knew what she was thinking! I can't help but smile every time I think of it.

The following day was Saturday. Cindy came up along with my daughter Chelsea and Cindy's mother. We took the elevator out to the main floor and out onto the street. We took a stroll to the Miracle Mile and spent some time at a mall. Chelsea climbed on my lap and I gave her rides through the hard floors of the mall. It was nice to be around her without my Halo.

It was incredible to get to see Chelsea. We had a great time. I would only see her every couple of weeks and I could see the changes in her each time. She was about to turn two, and she was growing quickly. When they finally left to go back home I felt sad. She was growing up and changing so quickly, and I wasn't there to see it. I knew I needed to stay in therapy and get as good as I could, but couldn't help but think of all I was missing out on. I wanted to be back home.

That Saturday night I went on another field trip. This time I went to a Chicago Bulls basketball game. Our group of about ten all got to sit right on the basketball floor in our wheelchairs. The "Love-a-bulls", the name of the Bulls' cheerleaders, were right alongside us and sometimes in front of us as they cheered on the players and fans. When there was a stop in the action, they occasionally would come over and talk with us. The game was great with the Bulls beating the Timberwolves. I think we all appreciated how sweet and nice the cheerleaders were to us as well. They went out of their way to be kind to all of us, and we all received a number of hugs before the game was over.

The following day was Sunday. Sunday was always a long, boring day. No therapy and a skeleton crew working the floor. Many patients were visiting their homes. It was just Tim and I in the room. Tim was a whole lot better than that first day they brought him in. Tim kept the nurses busy. He was like I was in the beginning. He hated to be in his bed, so he was constantly getting the nurses to transfer him into his chair. It took quite a few people to get Tim into his chair. He was thin, but quite tall. His injury kept him from being able to help with the transfer in any way.

I watched the previous week as he was being taught how to blow into his straw to work his monstrous chair. He was as bad of a driver as John was.

I would watch as he would start and stop again and again before he got his chair turned properly to pass through our doorway.

Tim talked in waves. His breath was shallow and his voice had a raspy, hollow sound. I'm sure that's not what his voice normally sounded like, but, like me, this spinal cord injury left him with a limited ability to breathe deeply. After only a few words, the breath would start running out and the last word or two would be soft and sometimes cut short until another breath could be taken and the sentence could be continued. I talked to Tim that whole afternoon in the main room where we normally ate.

I was able to press my hands against the sides of my wheelchair to lift my butt up off the cushion for a few seconds. These were called pressure release exercises and Kate my physical therapist would work with me on them. I usually did pressure releases every half an hour or so. Tim couldn't move his arms so he couldn't do such exercises. The nurses would recline him in his chair, but that didn't completely take the pressure off his butt, so he would have to be returned to his bed after a few hours. He would stay in bed for an hour or so then beg to get back in his chair. I knew exactly what he was going through. It's a terrible feeling when you can't move your body and you're stuck in one spot. The bed was a jail to him, just as it had been to me. A wheelchair offers mobility; maybe not as good as walking, but far better than being motionless in a bed.

I was still in the main room when they got Tim out of bed again. He came rolling out with his straw in his mouth. He rolled over to me and told me his family was on their way. Soon Tim was surrounded. His wife was next to him and a whole horde of kids were running around and on top of him. You could just see his face light up when his family was around. It seemed to me that Tim liked the simple things in life. I bet he was a great husband and father. He had such a laid back quality to his nature and loved his wife and kids very much. Eventually his nurse came by to get him back into bed. He delayed it a couple times, but finally he and his clan were headed back to the room.

I stayed out in the main room a little longer. I wanted to give Tim and his family some privacy, but I also didn't like being confined to bed. I finally went back to the room just as his kids were saying their goodbyes. Tim was on his back in bed.

The top of his bed was elevated. His arms and hands were placed neatly beside him. Once again his kids took turns climbing up on top of his lap and hugging him goodbye. He would do his best to lean his head forward as each kid kissed him on his cheek. The family had to leave so the nursing staff could get Tim and myself ready for bed. I watched as the last child gave Tim a big hug and scampered out the door. The family was staying at the Ronald McDonald house and would be back tomorrow.

I was by my bed with my back to Tim when I heard sounds coming from his direction. I pushed my chair over to the side of his bed and looked up at his face. Tim had huge tears rolling down his cheek and was sobbing uncontrollably. I said to Tim "Why are you crying? They will be coming back tomorrow!" I will never forget what he said to me. He said "I can handle being paralyzed and in a wheelchair for the rest of my life, but I can't handle not being able to hug my kids." I felt my own eyes glazing over, the moisture building up. I said "Your kids love you very much," but I didn't know what else to say. I had no thoughts on how to comfort Tim. There was a pause of about five seconds, but it seemed like an eternity, then the nurse entered the room and helped me into bed. I went to sleep that night with tears running down my cheeks as well, wondering why such a bad thing should happen to such a good person.

So many people believe in Karma. I had always believed in Karma. It just seems to make sense that Karma should exist. It seems like a fair way for life to operate, but I no longer believe in Karma. Very bad things can happen to some very good people, and some people who do very bad things sometimes experience no ill effects. I've seen so much, and I believe it's a crap shoot. There is no rhyme or reason! We find examples of Karma to fit our view and neglect those examples that don't. I, like most people, think Karma should exist, but I don't believe it does.

I had gotten so used to wearing that Halo for the past three months that sleeping without it was strange. Moving from one side to the other was significantly easier. I would just lock my wrist around the side rails on the bed and pull myself into position. I wanted to pull my body completely over till I was resting on my stomach, but it frightened me a little bit. I really wasn't sure what might happen. I might be stuck on my stomach the whole night and be unable to get back on my side.

I decided to wait and just sleep in a fetal position. It was strange to feel my head nestled on that soft pillow. My head hadn't touched a pillow since my Halo was put on.

My eyes opened slowly to a gleaming Jennifer staring down at me. What a difference it makes when you are continually showered with all this positive energy. All the little things we do, the positive energy we exude, the small tasks we do to help others make an incredible impact, not just on that person, but on the people that person makes contact with as well. I learned this lesson in those first few days. The day my nurse read me all those letters. Jennifer may not have known it, but she was getting me started each day to go out and succeed. To go work hard and believe, and to spend my day sharing the same smile with others that she was sharing with me.

I went to breakfast and had my usual bowl of cereal. Normally I would sit across from Josh and laugh my way through our morning meal, but he wasn't there that morning. I talked to quite a few people and then headed out to physical therapy a little early. Kate wasn't surprised to see my Halo off. I think she had known before me when I was getting it removed. Until now, the Halo had hindered many of the things that Kate wanted to work on. The first thing she wanted to do when she got me on the mat was to get me to my stomach. With help from Kate I was soon on my stomach, and just as I had expected, was unable to do much once I got there. My body didn't lay flat because my hips were so tight. There was an arch, as if I was purposely hiking my buttocks skyward. It doesn't take long for muscles to get tight and shorten.

Kate wanted to start working on my hips more. My hips hadn't had a proper stretch since I had been wearing the Halo. While lying on my stomach she helped prop my elbows up underneath my shoulders while she straddled me around my waist and put gentle pressure down on my hips. My hips were so incredibly tight that it was everything I could do to keep my elbows in place. This now became part of an everyday routine to loosen my hips up the best we could. In time I would work on lifting up on my elbows to progressively make the stretching more intense. We also worked on getting to my back from my stomach. It seems like such a simple thing to do, but when your arms are weak and the rest of your body is unable to help, a simple task like turning over is far more complicated than you would think.

Practicing with Kate eventually allowed me to sleep part of the night on my stomach, which was exactly Kate's goal. What better way to stretch my hips than to do it while I was asleep?

Rope therapy changed some, too. We had been working on straightening my legs and they had gotten significantly stronger. We had worked on sitting up from lying on my back, but that was something I hadn't been able to master. Until now, I didn't realize how much the Halo was limiting me, but the first time I tried to sit up without the Halo, I knew that in time I'd be successful. We also began working more on my hip flexors. I would lie on my stomach and with the aid of ropes attempt lifting my leg from a straightened position. My strength was very weak in my hips, nearly negligible, but she would spot me and help when she needed to. She also would pat repeatedly the muscles she wanted to contract. My body was constantly burning, and although the going was slow, there was never a moment when Kate didn't have things for me to work on.

My occupational therapist Melissa was also challenging me on an everyday basis. With the absence of the Halo she renewed her efforts in teaching me to put my shoes and socks on by myself. I was so limber at this time that I could have kissed my feet if I wanted to. The difficulty with socks was manipulating them with my hands. My strategy was to roll the top of the socks around my fingers and hopefully pull them over my feet. Putting on a pair of socks could take the better part of an hour, and as frustrating as it was for me, I've got to think it was equally frustrating for her. Once my socks were on, the shoes were relatively easy. I might drop my shoes a few times, but once they were over my toes it was just about wedging them back and forth till they slipped on and pulling the Velcro straps across.

RIC was really good about customizing your clothes to make it easier to get dressed on your own. My shoes were fitted with velcro straps. My pants had loops to help pull my pants up.

RIC had it's own kitchen. Melissa taught me to make many different dishes. She also taught me to use grabbers for retrieving things out of my reach. I can't say I didn't drop things constantly, but through repetition I eventually got things done. We worked on just about everything you could think of to prepare me to live independently.

I had been taking weightlifting class on Tuesdays and Thursdays, and now that my halo and vest were off I was able to add the swimming pool to my schedule on Mondays and Wednesdays. Anne, a therapist, would help me get changed into my swim trunks behind a pulled curtain. It was a small pool and I would normally have the pool to myself. The class was an hour long, but my actual time in the water was about thirty minutes. Once my swim trunks were on, Anne would roll me over to the side of the pool and help me transfer into a pool chair. My transfers were getting so good that I basically did it on my own while the therapist spotted me. The pool chair was then lowered into the pool.

This may sound strange, but sometimes I would forget how paralyzed I was. As the chair lowered into the pool, the water would slowly cover my feet and then legs, then chest, until the water reached my shoulders and arms. As I first began entering the water, my paralyzed body would sense the water and it seemed lukewarm, basically the same temperature as my body. Each body part felt the same as it was lowered into the water until the water reached my injury line. When the water touched the area that still had full feeling, I would realize that the water was actually very cold. It would happen this way each time I entered the pool, and it struck me as weird each and every time.

Anne would take me into her arms, much like you would cradle a baby. She would walk around the pool letting the water flow over my body. She would have me wrap my arms around her neck and straighten and close my legs. I would also work on straightening my legs on my own. Water is a wonderful way of strengthening the body without the added weight and friction. I would hold on to the side of the pool and let my lower body float out to the side. Anne had me do many small movements that were impossible outside the pool. Pool therapy became one of my favorite classes, and should be a lifetime therapy for anyone suffering a debilitating sickness or injury.

Making transfers had become much easier without the limiting effects of the halo. I found I could transfer from bed or mat to wheelchair without even using a transfer board if I placed my wheelchair close enough. I would put the wheelchair at about a forty-five degree angle and facing me. In a sitting position I would work my way to the edge of the bed as close to the wheelchair as possible without falling off.

I would then grab my legs and put them in a position that I would expect them to be after the transfer. I would reach out with my hand and wrap it around the far hand rest on the chair while my other hand, in a closed fist, would press off the bed or mat. My butt would then slip over to the chair. I needed to use a closed fist because I couldn't open my hand.

It probably took a week or so before I could convince the nurses in my room to allow me to transfer on my own. They always wanted to be there to observe. Once I had permission to do my own transfers I was free to go where I wanted without needing anyone's permission or help. This amount of freedom was a small but important step towards ultimate independence.

I hadn't seen Josh all day as I rolled into dinner. It had been a long Monday and I had put in a full eight hours of therapy. I was tired and was happy to see Josh. He always seemed to have a way of making me smile. It seemed obvious to me how he ended up getting into his motorcycle accident. He was a young man who was a risk taker. A person who liked the excitement of taking things to the brink, perhaps I enjoyed his company because I was like that myself. I saw him sitting at a table and went over and sat across from him.

It wasn't the same Josh I had grown accustomed to. He seemed sad and although he said hi, he didn't seem to want to talk much. I sensed he needed his space and began eating my meal in silence. Once we were finished eating he looked over at me and said, "Matt died!" Matt, the young kid who had just gotten discharged only a couple of weeks earlier. I couldn't believe it. Josh and Matt had been roommates down the hall. Matt had given Josh his contact information before he left that day with his mother. Eventually Josh explained to me what had happened. He didn't know many of the details, but he told me the best he could.

Matt had gotten sick while staying with his mother at their home. He had been in bed, presumably on his back, when his throat filled up with fluid. He ended up being unable to roll over and clear his throat. He drowned during the night. It had happened over the weekend.

My first thoughts went to Tim that first night when Tim was struggling to breathe, and then my mind imagined the intense pain that Matt's mother must be going through. She loved her son so much. She had to be devastated.

I never saw Matt's father and I assumed he wasn't a part of his life. It seemed that Matt was everything to his mother. I wondered if she felt any guilt for his death. I assume that she did. A heavy cloud hung over me for the rest of the day that I couldn't shake. I couldn't help but think of how sad his mother certainly was and how lonely she was going to be.

Life really is "like a box of chocolates." We never really know what we're going to get. I think of Matt, and he taught me a lesson. We all have times when we must rely on others, but ultimately we need to put ourselves in position to rely on ourselves. This is what makes having a spinal cord injury so difficult. Someone like Tim is forced to rely on others for most everything, but you still need to have goals. It may be walking, but it might be something as simple as breathing on your own so you don't need to rely on a machine.

One thing all spinal cord injured people share is the need to find solace with their situation. I by no means am saying you should be satisfied with your situation, because you can always find ways to improve, but accept your accomplishments as well as your setbacks. Work hard, maintain hope, be patient, and go as far as your injury and your mind can take you.

CHAPTER ELEVEN
Life Without A Halo

It was Tuesday morning and I still had a full week of therapies ahead of me. I was putting in eight hours of classes a day, which was the most I was allowed to take. Jennifer, her bright light cascading over my damaged body, was starting with my bed this fine morning. Another nurse was taking care of my roommates, so I had Jen all to myself.

I was getting better at using my hands, but much of my improvement came from strengthening what I already had rather than a return of movement from a healing spinal cord. I was also getting much better at manipulating my hands through flexing my wrist. When you lift your wrist the hand will close and when you lower your wrist, it opens.

After taking my vitals it was time for my morning cath; the large plastic jug that looked like a glorified measuring cup, the soft, orange catheter still in its' sterile package, and a tube of lubricant. Jen raised my bed into a sitting position. I sat there and once again realized what a difference it was to be without that cumbersome halo and vest. I could actually look down and see my lower body. It was good to see that everything was still in good shape down there. I wasn't so sure after my debacle with what I thought was the remote control cord during those first few weeks. It still makes me a bit nauseous thinking about it.

Jennifer laid out the supplies on my hospital table. I transferred into my wheelchair with Jennifer inches away, prepared to catch me if I had any trouble. Transferring on my own was still new to me, so I was overly cautious. Jen had me wheel over to the sink and wash my hands with soap and water. We rolled back to my table where the supplies were setting. Jennifer was going to have me catheterize myself today.

It would have been better had I worn sterile gloves like Jen, but it was also painfully obvious that my hands weren't ready to put on gloves. My hands were in a constant, partially clinched fist. I couldn't fully open them and even if I could, I wouldn't have been able to grip the glove with the opposite hand to pull them on. Jen was good at what she did. She knew gloves weren't a viable option, so washing my hands would have to be good enough.

Jennifer had been teaching me here and there, and I knew what to do. I opened the plastic package, pulled the catheter out, and laid it down on the outside of the plastic wrapping it came in. I then took the tube of lubricant, and using the heels of both my hands, pressed the tube till a huge gob smothered one end of the catheter. Three more globs later I had the catheter covered with about five times more lube than I actually needed.

Now for the tough part! I couldn't thread a needle when I had full use of my hands, so this was going to be a challenging task. My hands were a shadow of what they once were. I grabbed hold of the catheter with my thumb and pointer finger and eventually got it threaded and sliding down my penis. The extra lubricant was building up at the tip forming an increasingly large mound as I slid the catheter deeper. I needed to have the outer part of the catheter over the top of the plastic jug before pressing the catheter pass my sphincter, otherwise there would be quite a mess once the urine started pouring out.

With some minor help I did a decent job for the first time. I would now be in charge of all my catheterizing. I would drop lubed catheters on the floor often. Occasionally the end of the catheter would fall out of the jug in full stream causing a mess, but like everything, you figure out the best way to do things and you get better. I rarely ever tried to do this from my wheelchair. I found sitting up in my bed with jug on the mattress situated between my knees was the way to go. I would leave the partially filled jug on my side table and periodically a nurse would come by write down the amount on a clipboard and empty the jug in the toilet.

At breakfast that morning I sat across from Josh, Karen, and Shelley, the two young girls using power wheelchairs. A new patient was at the table as well. Her name was Vicky and she was there with her husband. Vicky was in her mid forties. She had light red hair, which from her darkened roots was most likely colored.

She was heavyset and reminded me of a stereotypical mother figure being thrown into a wheelchair. She had use of her arms and hands, and appeared to have a high back injury. She was in a manual wheelchair and her husband had pushed her up to our table. It was the same scenario that I had been seeing over and over. New patients in their first few days with loved ones at their side. The look of concern on their faces as they tended to their fallen. That look of being lost, not knowing what to expect for the future. Wondering to themselves, "Is this how life is going to be from now on?"

Her husband had many questions for me. I answered each one the best I could. I wish I could have answered all his questions, but some were questions I was asking as well. I did tell him things would get better and they would. The doctors always seem to paint the bleakest picture possible, but you can't always believe what the doctors tell you. You have to believe things will get better. "How much better?" Well! That was one of those questions I was asking, but I knew it would get better than what it was now.

Kate and Melissa had me for a couple of hours apiece. They both did their usual magnificent jobs. They challenged me to do things I didn't think I could do. Kate continued the rope therapy and my movements were getting stronger and more profound. I was increasingly able to move parts of my body with less of an effort mentally. I would close my eyes and imagine the part of my body I wanted to move. My brain was getting used to how it had to think to make my body move. Whether true or not, I felt I was re-wiring my spinal cord.

Melissa was helping me out of my wheelchair and onto the ground. She gave me ideas on ways to pull myself up from the ground and into a chair, sofa or my wheelchair. In the beginning I couldn't accomplish these tasks, but she kept making me try. Each day I would get closer. I believe she knew I'd eventually be able to accomplish her tasks. I wanted to believe as well, but it would be a lie if I said doubt never crept into my mind. My mind and its' ability to focus was getting stronger and stronger. I could have used this strength in sports growing up, I thought, but sports were just games and this was my life. My commitment and focus was better than it ever had been. I would tell myself continually "I can do this!"

Rehabilitation is about perseverance regardless of how small the improvement. If you have a bad day, you come back the next with renewed determination and a positive mindset. Jim Valvano got it right when he said "Don't give up, don't ever give up!"

RIC never missed a chance at preparing me for the outside world. In place of an occupational class they added a writing class. We gathered at tables, still in our wheelchairs. Some could hold pencils, but unfortunately I couldn't. I was given a pencil holder that slipped over my finger. I placed it over my pointer finger and tried to write. Writing was completely different than what it used to be. My fingers couldn't move independently so resting my hand on the paper as I wrote left me unable to move my pencil. I soon found that I had to keep my hand in the air and move my entire hand and arm. Well! If you've ever tried writing with your hand in the air and moving your arm, you'll see just how bad you're handwriting becomes. Add to that the fact that my arms were still recovering from my injury, and you're left with something that rivals that of a chicken scratch. I would just concentrate on trying to make it legible.

A man named Joseph sat next to me and soon we started a conversation. Joseph had black, short hair and was fairly short. He had full function of his hands and although he was in a wheelchair he could walk. He made numerous short trips to get more supplies walking each time. His gait was labored and I could tell it was difficult for him. His legs were weak, but he preferred to walk whenever he could.

Conversations back in college tended to eventually get to "What's your major?" In Rehab it always seemed to go to "What happened to you?" His situation was different than anyone else that I had met. He didn't suffer an injury. He had a degenerative spine disease and was continually getting worse. A few months earlier he said he was walking around normally, but now his body was getting weaker with every passing day. He admitted himself into RIC in hopes of slowing down the process.

We had our writing class once a week. In three weeks I would come to class and he could no longer walk or write. He was worse than I was. It made me think about how I had everything taken away in a blink of an eye, but now I was slowly re-capturing some of what I lost.

He would watch his condition get continually worse with apparently no chance of ever getting better. It made me realize that there are many things in life worse than my situation. I really never went through a "Why me?" phase, and it might have been because of people like Joseph and Tim and many others who had it much worse than me. I did say a few times, however, "Why them?"

During the course of the day I ran into Vicky. Vicky was waiting for her next physical therapy class. I could tell there was something wrong with her. She acted confused and slurred her words as if she was drunk. I had seen this before growing up. My mother was always worried about her health and many times taking multiple medications. One time she had similar symptoms from mixing her medications. I was able to talk to Vicky's therapist alone and tell her something was wrong with her and it may be because of her medications. The following day she was fine. It had been an adverse effect of her medications. I'm sure they would have caught it without me, but it felt good to know that I brought it to their attention.

Friday night I went on one of the RIC outings. We went to the movie theater. The group decided on the movie "The Man Without A Face". This wasn't the type of movie I would have normally gone to before my accident. It was about a man who was formerly a teacher. His face was disfigured on one side. He reaches out to help a young boy, but is wrongly accused of being a pedophile by the town's people. The people thought he was a freak because of his disfigurement. I cried! I was a different person after my accident. I was far more empathetic and felt the pain of others. I felt this man's pain not just from the wrongful accusations, but from the people judging him based on his appearance. I'm still not sure if I cried for him or partly for myself. RIC was a protected environment where everyone had visible problems. When the time came for me to leave RIC I would be working with kids year-round. How will they react to being taught by someone in a wheelchair? I would mentally prepare myself daily for kids judging me. If it happened, I wanted to be strong and not let it affect me.

Cindy picked me up the following week to take me home for Thanksgiving. It's amazing how easy it was to get into the car without the halo. I was able to scoot around in the seat without my halo and the trip was very pleasant.

When we arrived home I was treated to a nice surprise. A lift was installed in the back yard that allowed me access to both floors of my split-level house. The lift was really more of a freight elevator. It was plenty large enough for my wheelchair, and even one or two extra people. You had to keep a green button pushed down until you reached your floor. The elevator would only work if the doors were closed. A small deck was built in the back and a sidewalk leading from the driveway to the elevator. It was a major undertaking of love from some volunteers in the town I lived in. All the labor and the majority of the materials were donated. I could now enter the basement or the main floor. A bathroom was in the basement along with a nice comfy couch that doubled as my bed.

The next couple of days were spent seeing all my family. It was especially nice to see my mother and father, whose health hadn't allowed them to come to Chicago to visit me. The food at RIC was very good, but what can beat homemade turkey and everything that goes with it? It was just the shot in the arm I needed. Regardless of all the wonderful people I had met in therapy, it would get lonely when I didn't get to see family. I knew when getting dropped off in Chicago a few days later that Christmas was coming up, and in four short weeks I'd be going home again.

It was Sunday night. I was dressed in just a gown and given a suppository. I liked to have my suppository early because I so hated Digistim. I wanted to give myself as much time as possible to go on my own. After the nurse rolled me to my side and inserted the suppository, she helped me into my shower chair and place a lined bucket below it. I sat there waiting for nature to run its course. The curtains were drawn. My gown was draped down to my knees. I heard a woman's voice, and moments later a little old lady popped her head through my curtain. She was small and frail, in her seventies with short, curly gray hair. I recognized her from the church I sometimes went to. I really didn't know her all that well, but the church had been praying for me weekly and she decided on a whim to come and visit me. I was completely touched, but at the same time torn. I wasn't sure how long she planned on staying. I truly wanted to give her as much of my time as possible, but at the same time, I was sitting with nothing but a robe on having just been given a suppository. Normally in this situation I am hoping to get some quick results and typically when things get moving it's not a quiet thing.

Now, I'm sitting here hoping it takes its' time until she leaves. Making matters worse was the fact she was clueless to my current situation. She was asking me about my stay here, what I had been doing, and never taking the time to look at the bucket under my chair or the fact I was in just a robe and on a shower chair. I normally would have loved every minute of her visit, but I couldn't help but think about what may happen at any moment and how embarrassing it was going to be. It's surprising that I felt that way. I thought all my modesty was gone! I guess it was because it was this sweet lady from church who came to visit me. She was sheltered from the world I was living in. She still lived by the same rules the outside world had. I somehow made it through her visit without anything embarrassing happening.

When she finally did walk out of my room it was only minutes later that everything came to fruition. It was every bit as loud as expected. I was so happy to have it over with, and even more happy to have it happen after she left.

The next four weeks of therapy were intense. I was able to get myself off the ground and into a sofa and a chair. I could even get into my chair, but that sometimes took me quite a while. I would pull myself to the chair, click on the brakes, and situate myself so that my back was against the front of the chair. While resting one elbow on the seat of the chair, my other arm would pull both of my legs into my body. At this point, my body was precariously unbalanced so success relied on using the wheelchair. My elbow would press into the chair while my other hand would grab the opposite hand-rest, pressing up on the hand-rest so that my butt would slide onto the seat.

In physical therapy we were working intensely on strengthening my hip muscles. I would need them if I ever hoped to take steps. I worked hard on straightening and closing my legs as well as spreading my legs apart and closing them using adductors and abductors. Closing them was much easier than opening them because many of my spasms involved my legs snapping shut. Kate would also routinely hook my muscles up to biofeedback machines to help me understand how my thinking was effecting muscle contractions.

The therapists in charge of wheelchair classes were taking us on hills to strengthen our arms, and we even had a race between the patients one day.

I would exercise my legs in the pool and I even learned how to wedge a pencil between my first and second fingers so that I could write without a pencil adapter. This technique also helped with using eating utensils.

A few weeks before Christmas, Kate was putting me through many of the same exercises. I could tell she was very happy with the progress we were making. All my movements had grown bigger and stronger. I still spent all my time on the mat; sometimes connected to ropes, sometimes not. As my legs continued to strengthen, Kate would occasionally break out the leg braces and place them on my legs. Leg braces are usually made of metal, but any strong material would work. They fit over your entire leg and lock out your knees to keep your legs straight. She would take me between the parallel bars and help me get into a standing position. I would work on rocking my hips from side to side, causing the legs to swing forward. Braces will work for anyone who has a strong upper body. No strength was needed in the legs.

The next day, Kate and I were about thirty minutes into a two-hour therapy session. I was still on the mat, having just received some needed stretching. Kate suddenly sat on the edge of the mat and paused. I knew her well enough. She was brainstorming on what to do next. She walked off and came back with a Physical Therapy Assistant. Kate strapped a gait belt to my waist and had me transfer into my wheelchair. We went over to the parallel bars where she adjusted them for my height. I was six foot three, so the bars usually needed to be raised.

Kate grabbed underneath one arm and the assistant the other. They lifted me up into standing position, which was unexpected because I didn't have my leg braces on. I grabbed the bars on both sides of me. She wanted to see if I could lock my legs straight while holding myself up with my arms.

My whole passion since my accident was for that first moment when I could prove my doctor and everyone wrong and stand for the first time. I imagined it nightly as I'd lay there with my eyes closed, seeing my body healing. I thought that I would just stand up directly out of my chair one day and start walking around just as I used to do. I was naïve, it doesn't work that way.

My arms had become very strong with all the weight lifting and pushing my chair all day. I could take the majority of my weight off my legs by holding onto the parallel bars and lifting with my arms.

I tried to straighten my legs, and to my surprise, I straightened and locked them and stood straight up. My arms were still supporting most of my weight, but I was standing up in the parallel bars and my legs were also bearing some of my weight.

My eyes got wet and tears were rolling down my cheeks. I mention the tears because it's important to realize I wasn't the same person who always had to be strong. I didn't have to be like my father, who never showed weakness or emotion. I had become vulnerable, and now I was beginning to overcome a seemingly impenetrable barrier. Crying is not a sign of weakness and the lack thereof isn't a sign of strength. Strength is having the guts to go after your goals and to stand by what you believe. Strength is raising a child. Strength is a lot of things and at that moment, strength was standing between those parallel bars and feeling the weight on my legs. I remember standing there and looking at all patients on their mats with therapists helping them. It was so strange to see them from this completely different perspective. The world looked a lot different while standing than it did from my wheelchair. I don't know what else to say, other than it's not the same. It was this moment that I will never forget for the rest of my life, looking out over the rehabilitation room while standing between those bars.

I spent the rest of our therapy standing for a minute or so and then collapsing back into my chair. I attempted to take steps and took a few small ones, but that was still a project that needed some work. I was surprised by the fact that I didn't think I was strong enough to stand, but I was. I doubted myself. I felt I had always been thinking as positive as possible, but there must have been lingering doubts hiding in the dark recesses of my psyche. This helped me lose some of these doubts. I was going to do my best not to doubt myself anymore.

For the next ten days I worked hard on standing inside the parallel bars and attempting to take steps. I was improving, but improvement always seemed slower than I hoped. One day I had three very special visitors. It was three of my best friends growing up. Randy had come down from Texas along with Burl, Paul and Randy's girlfriend. These were three guys I had played basketball with on a regular basis and were good friends off the court too. I didn't know Randy's girlfriend, but she was an attractive girl who besides her regular job would sometimes work as a ring girl in boxing bouts.

Their timing was impeccable. They all showed up at my Physical Therapy class just as I was getting my leg braces strapped on. These braces only reached to just above my calf muscles and were designed to help support my ankles, which were still very weak.

This was my first attempt to try standing and taking steps outside of the parallel bars. I was privy to three therapists this time. Kate had a walker ready for me. I had a therapist in front and behind me in case I were to fall, I think having some of my best friends there to watch motivated me and got my adrenaline going. I stood up and looked out across the room. It was a huge room. Once I got to my feet, Kate held tightly to the gait belt wrapped around my waist, with all my strength, I nudged a foot forward a few inches and then rested. I then did the same with my other foot. My arms helped me with every step I took. I would use my arms to twist my upper body while simultaneously focusing on pushing my feet forward. They were small steps and I may not have gone far but I took seventeen steps with my walker that day.

I think my friends were stunned. I hadn't let on to anyone that I had stood a few days earlier. I wanted to get better before I told anyone. The word in the outside world was that I was paralyzed and would never walk again. When the braces were off and my hour was done, my friends gathered around me. It seemed just like the old days. They were pumped over seeing me walk. It was a scene I don't think they were expecting. I could see their excitement! I, on the other hand, was completely exhausted, but at the same time pretty stoked myself.

At the end of the day we all went out for dinner. It was one of the nicer days I had had since my accident. They all spent the night. The next day was Saturday and we spent the entire day together. I couldn't help but laugh when Randy's girlfriend was freezing. She had lived in Texas and didn't know Chicago in December. We'd be walking between the buildings, and the frigid wind would blast into our faces. It's not something you find in Texas, that's for sure!

CHAPTER TWELVE
Christmas Time

We were going to have an extended vacation from therapy during the Christmas Holidays. Most of the patients were gearing up to get out of RIC and head back home.

We were at dinner on Thursday, only a couple of days before our holiday break. The room was packed and we had a special Christmas meal with all the extras. There was going to be therapy tomorrow, but many patients who lived far away were going to miss dinner tomorrow so we were having our Holiday meal today.

I was sitting with Tim. Tim's family wasn't coming to visit him today because they were preparing his house so they could pick him up tomorrow. He was excited to be going home, and to get a chance to see his farm. I don't remember him being home since I met him. I'm sure it will bring back memories, especially since that's where he was hurt. Tim had an amazing way of staying positive, especially around others, but there were also those moments when I could see the sadness in his face. There was also a fear; the fear of the unknown. "What does my life hold for me?" "What kind of burden will I have on my family?" And of course, the question that creeps into most of our thoughts from time to time "Would it have been better had I died?" The thought crossed my mind from time to time, but I was very grateful to be alive.

Tim was truly happy today. I could see the light in his face. He was looking forward to leaving with his family tomorrow. He wasn't sure just how early he would be able to leave the next day and he wanted to find out. Across the room was the administrative office. It looked out onto the cafeteria much like the nurses station in "One Flew Over The Cuckoos Nest" looked out over the treatment room.

There was a long counter and behind it a hub of activity with nurses and secretaries and others all going about there business. Tim was in his monstrously huge and heavy tank of a chair. He decided he was going to ask the office across the room and see if they knew. His chair was facing the counter. I watched as his mouth opened and his tongue slithered out and pulled the straw to his lips. In a few moments, his beast of a chair was traveling briskly towards the counter. No sooner had he started, the straw slipped out from his lips. The chair continued barreling towards the counter as he tried desperately to grab it back with his tongue, but it was just out of reach.

It seemed like slow motion as Tim screamed to the people working behind the counter to look out. The chair crushed into the counter as workers, mostly middle-aged women with eyes bulging, went scurrying around their desks. It didn't end there. As Tim and his chair slammed into the counter, his chair bounced back and slammed it again. After numerous collisions, one of the ladies behind the counter finally got to his chair and got it stopped. There was some damage to the counter. There was a momentary blank stare by Tim and then he broke into his light, raspy laugh that was completely addictive. I began laughing along with just about the whole room. The one person I noticed who wasn't laughing was the woman who turned Tim's chair off. She still looked a bit shaken.

The following day was a quiet day in therapy. Many of the patients had already left for their Christmas vacations and there was just a feeling in the air of the upcoming break, even from the therapists. It reminded me of those last couple of days of grade school when everyone seemed less intense, or the last few feet of a race when runners start to relax just before hitting the finish line.

I spent that night as the only one left in my room. It was strangely quiet. I had grown accustomed to all the activity involved when nurses were getting us all ready for bed.

The following morning it was my turn to head home. Christmas eve was spent at my parent's house. We had the whole immediate family and their children there. Christmas get-togethers had always given me a sense of family and togetherness. I arrived at my parent's home early and transferred onto the sofa. One by one members of the family would come through the door.

Each person would make a point to come over and talk. I don't know why, but I felt a feeling of disconnect. I had been in the hospital for four and half months by now. It seems silly, but I felt almost like a guest. It had nothing to do with my family, who were amazing, but it was from inside me. I guess it was because everything was so different. I had been gone so long, and now I was here on the sofa unable to physically participate in the festivities. I sat as everyone moved about the room with ease. I just stayed on the sofa. When time came to eat, I needed someone to make a plate for me. It seemed everyone's lives had changed so much in the past months, and I hadn't been a part of it. My daughter was sitting on my lap and was growing every day. It was surreal as I watched her take packages to people in the room. In our family, it was the youngest child who was in charge of handing out presents, and at nearly two years old, that was my daughter Chelsea.

The following day we went to Cindy's parents house for Christmas Day. I got to see her brother, who was my old doubles partner from my tennis days. I again sat on the sofa. It was just an unusual feeling being surrounded by all able bodied people with no visible physical handicaps. It wasn't the world that I had grown accustomed to.

The following day we headed back to Chicago. I didn't want to return so soon, but that's what was decided. I'm not sure why I needed to head back so soon, but I didn't question it. I was thankful to have spent three days with my family and friends. There may have been times when I felt out of place, but that was my problem. Everyone did their best to make me feel at home during my stay, it was just myself trying to adapt to a world away from the "Island of Misfit Toys."

When I entered the Rehab floor it was quiet and empty with just a skeleton crew walking around. I entered my room and it was empty. All of my roommates were still out with their families for the holidays. I felt a deep sadness that night when I went to bed. I had been injured for five months, but never really had a bout with depression. Both Genesis and RIC tried their best to line me up with a psychologist. It was protocol for patients like this, but I refused to see anyone. They assume depression is inevitable, but I had never been depressed. I may have had moments of sadness, but nothing that lasted. I was never prone to depression my entire life.

I just started to stand and take steps so I should be happy, but now I felt this enormous sadness envelope me.

I woke up the next morning to an empty room. A nurse I had never seen came into my room and performed her duties. There was no therapy for the week, so there was no need to get out of bed. The next few days were all the same. I would lie in bed for almost the entire day. I ate very little and didn't feel like doing anything. As I lay in bed, spasms would rock my body. My stomach would lock, my legs would fly up, and my ankles would force my feet into a ballet like pose. If I could re-live these days, I surely would. My inactivity, along with the spasm in my ankles, contributed to my developing Foot Drop, a condition where the muscle in the Achilles Heel shorten and causes the feet to droop. Intense stretching couldn't get rid of it, and it has a major impact on your ability to walk. Half leg braces can hold the foot up, but I wanted to be brace free. The next four days found me truly sad. I knew what I needed. I needed to get back to work. Growing up as a child, I would always play sports or go running when I was feeling down. I loved to feel the rush of endorphins. Activities gave me something other than my problems to focus on.

The room remained empty until New Years Eve. That morning, Tim returned to the room. Tim and I had breakfast together. His wife helped feed him. Tim had returned with his wife, her sister, and brother-in-law. They had a hotel room and were going out that night for New Years Eve. They asked me if I'd like to come along. I said "Of course!" She left for the hotel room and Tim and I stayed and talked for a while. Eventually Tim wanted to go downstairs and left for the elevators. I headed back to my room and watched TV from the small adjustable set above my bed.

It was quite a while, more than an hour, when Tim finally returned to the room. He had this gigantic grin on his face. Tim had this smile that made anyone that saw it smile as well. He looked like a small child who got his fingers caught in the cookie jar. I looked up at him with a smile and said "Tim where have you been?" He said "In the elevator." I looked at him somewhat puzzled, "I rolled my wheelchair into an open elevator. I noticed there wasn't anyone running the elevator as the doors closed. I was stuck there until someone finally pushed the button."

I started laughing, and at the time I needed a good laugh. Tim was laughing too. That hollow, raspy laugh just made it all the more funny. I pictured Tim sitting patiently in his elevator wondering when someone would come along and open the doors. Because it was so dead, it took more than an hour. I know there are some that may think it unkind to laugh at such a thing, but we both found humor in it. You need to be able to laugh, even at yourself from time to time. Taking yourself too seriously can make it all the more difficult to get by day to day.

That evening Tim, his wife, his sister-in-law and her husband came into the room to get Tim ready. We left at around 6PM and didn't mention to the nurses that we were planning on staying out late in case the staff had problems with it. We headed over to their hotel room, where they had beer and wine and some New Years Eve hats and such. We spent much of the time amidst many other people in the lobby area of the motel. I hadn't had any alcohol since my accident and really wasn't in the mood to drink, but to celebrate the evening I ended up having three beers during the course of the night. Tim had quite a few more than me and had to have his leg bag emptied out by his wife more than once.

Tim was as happy as I'd ever seen him. How amazing it seemed to me, that he could always seem so happy despite the fact he wasn't able to move anything from his neck down. But he was.

Tim hadn't gotten any return of movement at all, and it was becoming increasingly evident that he probably wouldn't. I, on the other hand, was improving on a daily basis. I felt guilty about my ability to walk when I was around Tim. I made sure never to mention it to him. I know he would have been sincerely happy for me, but I had a gut feeling it would hurt him, so I kept it to myself.

We celebrated the coming of a new year with a large group outside our hotel. It was a lot of fun. It was snowing lightly as we headed back to RIC and we talked about our strategy once we arrived at our floor. We knew we'd be in trouble and the staff would be upset with us for coming back so late, so we formulated a plan.

We planned to quietly roll to our room. Tim had three people to help him into bed and I could get into bed by myself. The elevator doors opened and we looked down the hall. It was empty.

The five of us quietly moved down the hall and towards our room. Just as we reached our door, Tim was maneuvering his chair with his straw when he glanced back at me and started his addictive chuckle. He was looking behind me, and I couldn't think of what was so funny. I turned my chair around and it became painfully obvious! Each night, maintenance would polish the floors until they shined. I looked down the hall and there were four muddy, wet tire tracks leading from the elevator and down the hall to our door. We entered our room, but we knew what was coming, and it only took a matter of seconds. It didn't take a bloodhound to find our trail and track it to our door, and we had a very unhappy nurse in our room only moments after arriving. She was still expressing her unhappiness to Tim's family as I transferred into bed. Funny thing about being paralyzed is you tend to get overlooked when it comes to blame. The nurse blamed Tim's family for our late night rendezvous and let us off the hook.

I pulled my curtain shut because I was anxious to catheterize myself. It had been about six hours and I had consumed those three beers. I got my clothes off and pulled the covers down to my ankles so that I was sitting up on just a sheet. I had my catheter and my jug and was preparing to use the lubrication when I could feel an intense urge to pee. It reminded me of those times, particularly when drinking, when you hold it until the bladder is about to burst. When you finally get to the bathroom you just close your eyes and relax. You feel a complete sense of relief as the stream flows out from your body. I closed my eyes and tried to re-capture that relaxed mindset. I focused on my genitals and tried to concentrate on relaxing my body the way I had done all my life.

My focus was so much better than it ever had been and I put all my energy towards opening my sphincter. I instinctively began massaging my stomach and suddenly a stream of urine erupted like a volcano out from my body and all over my legs and bed. It lasted about five seconds. I created a wet spot on my sheets and mattress the size of a plate. I grabbed the jug and tried to pee some more into it, but couldn't seem to do it. I catheterized myself and put the full jug on the table.

Once Tim was taken care of, the nurse came over to my bed. She was still angry, and when she saw my bed she became a little angrier. I, on the other hand, was elated.

I wasn't happy I peed my bed, but if I could pee on my own, this was every bit as important as walking. After she cleaned me up, I transferred into my chair. Maintenance brought in a new mattress and my nurse dressed my bed with new sheets. I had a good night's sleep. Whether it was the beer, the ability to pee, or just having fun for the first time in a week, all I know is that I slept well.

CHAPTER THIRTEEN
A New Year

New Years Day was a Saturday, and RIC had an excellent meal for the few of us that were still there. During the course of the weekend more and more patients were returning. I used to love watching football on New Years Day. I would watch Bowl games from morning till night, but I had little desire to watch them now. I found sports as being far less important than before my injury. I looked upon it with different eyes. The little that I did see just made me think how silly it was for all these people to take a game so seriously.

There were a couple of nurses I knew who worked the pediatric floor, so I spent part of Sunday playing with kids in wheelchairs. I think I did it as much for myself as for them. Seeing all these young kids struck down at such a young age made me appreciate the fact I was thirty-two when I got hurt. It was amazing to see how resilient kids can be. In many ways, they are more resilient than adults. They had a playroom and it was nice that the nurses allowed me to play catch with them. I'd throw the beach ball and they'd laugh as they tried to catch it. I saw children who were strong enough to pull themselves around with their arms on the mat, and then there were the most unfortunate ones who were much like Tim. It was another moment that allowed me to see all the wonderful things I still had in my life and to be appreciative for it.

It's all a matter of perspective. The millionaire who grumbles because his stocks went down are on one end, all the way on the other end is the child who moves their wheelchair by blowing into a straw. Even that child can find others worse off than themselves if they look hard enough.

At the end of WWII U.S. troops forced German citizens to walk through the concentration camps so they would see the innocent Jews who were killed and tossed into piles by the Nazis.

I think it was a powerful thing to do. Seeing tragedy on TV or reading about it in the newspaper doesn't have the same effect as seeing it in person. Anyone who can't seem to appreciate the wonderful things in their life should go and visit a place like RIC, look at the children, and realize life could be much worse. Gratitude is a wonderful thing, a truly wonderful thing.

On Monday I had my full day of therapy again. I was excited to get back to work. My physical therapy consisted of strengthening my body through rope therapy and walking with a walker. Kate had made an appointment with prosthetics, and I went to their office to get fitted for leg braces that went just above the calf. These would be similar to the ones I was using, but be specifically sized to fit my legs. They were made of molded plastic and velcro straps. My Foot-drop on my right ankle made the brace cut into my calf, but other than that they were lighter and fit better than the generic braces. I could walk just a little farther and lift my legs a little higher than before. Kate was always stressing lifting my knees as I walked. My muscles were still very weak and after a few steps they would begin to tire. The first muscles to fatigue were my quadriceps. When they got tired I would begin dragging my feet rather than lifting them. Kate spent more time on my quality of walking than she did the distance. We still spent some of our time between the parallel bars for that very reason. It was much easier to keep my posture straight and lift my legs there than in a walker.

Melissa still had me in the Stander everyday. I had gotten to where I could get into just about anything from the ground. I could transfer into the shower chair and bathe myself. I was working on buttoning my shirt, which was difficult and time consuming, but given enough time I could do.

A new class was added to my routine. For a couple of days a week I would be taking a Driving class. I needed to learn to drive a vehicle by using hand controls. I also needed the certificate to renew my license when I was released. The instructor taught me how to use the various controls. The steering wheel was fitted with a rotating knob that I could use to help hold onto the wheel. My left hand would press down on a handle to press the gas and push in on the same handle to press the brake. We spent the first few days in a parking garage and parking lots, but eventually we took to the streets. Lucky me, getting to learn how to drive in downtown Chicago!

You just have to love the way the Taxicabs zip in and around you all the time. Then there's the "Lake Effect" snow that adds a little more drama to the situation. I got through the classes without an accident and received my certificate showing that I went through the class. My depression was far behind me. I was working too hard and feeling too tired each day to feel sorry for myself.

On Thursday I was sitting with Josh for dinner, the teenager who had a bit of a wild streak in him. He was getting released in a few days, and I was getting out in about a week. He had hatched a plan with the two teenage girls he hung out with. They each had power wheelchairs and he had gotten permission to borrow them after they went to bed on Friday. He wanted me to go with him to Hooters on Friday and use these two power wheelchairs to get there. Hooters was only about a mile straight down the road and we had these two power wheelchairs. What could go wrong? I thought, "Of course I'll go with him."

We waited until after medications were given and the girls were put to bed. I was able to transfer into the power wheelchair and Josh got help from one of the attendants. I'm still not sure if the attendant knew the plan, or was just blindly helping Josh out, but Josh got himself into the wheelchair and we were ready to go. We had both spent the day indoors taking therapy, and were a bit surprised when we reached the first floor and rolled out the door. Whether it was lake effect snow or just a good old weather front coming through, there was a good three or four inches of fresh snow on the ground and it was still coming down hard. The weather wasn't all that bad, probably in the 20s or 30s and no wind to speak of. The snow was the heavy packing kind; the kind you loved as a kid because you could pack it and have snowball fights or make an awesome snowman. We had both checked our battery levels and they read as full. The girls had gotten to bed early just so we could get fully charged vehicles for our trip.

We took the elevators down to ground floor and powered our way through to the sidewalk outside. It had been snowing throughout the day and night. The air was crisp and clean. What a beautiful sight to see as the light, airy snowflakes drifted silently through the air. The streets were strangely absent of traffic and the sidewalks were empty. The streetlights reflected off all the dropping snow and the whole world seemed quieter than normal. It was almost like stepping into a dream.

It looked like about six inches of fluffy white snow had fallen. There were very few prints in the snow, which for Chicago was not only unusual, but also a little eerie. It really did have the feeling that we had just been transported to another realm, where noise and bustle didn't exist. A tranquil place where all your troubles melted away. I sat, mesmerized, with the subtle light show as each dropping flake twinkled as it fell. The snow that had settled on the sidewalk was just as beautiful as it reflected light into a billion small brilliant crystals.

I guess Josh didn't appreciate the night quite as much as me, because he was already trudging through the heavy snow leaving two pronounced tracks with his heavy chair. It seemed that Josh was on a mission and taking time to look at this amazing night was not on his agenda. I pushed my controller, my chair lurched forward, and I was soon following Josh's trail.

The problem with freshly falling snow at night, especially when it's as heavy as this was, is that it has a way of tricking the eye so that you have trouble discerning depth. I was surprised that Josh was full throttle down the sidewalk because I had trouble seeing where the sidewalk ended and the curb began. It'd be nice to think that each and every curb had a gently slanting slope that would lead wheelchairs gently to the road, but having been on these sidewalks in the daytime, I knew that wasn't the case. You can go plenty of blocks in downtown Chicago and find wheelchair ramps at each corner and then for no reason find yourself looking at a curb with a hefty drop. Curbs in Chicago are formidable and need to be handled with care. In my regular wheelchair, going over a curb of this height without doing a wheelie first would result in lying face down in the road, and if you wore a seatbelt you'd probably have your wheelchair on your back as well.

We had both been on the sidewalks of Chicago, but neither of us had ever been this way. It amazed me how much faith Josh had at each and every corner that there would be a ramp. We were in heavy, motorized chairs. Perhaps there would be no ill effects barreling off a steep curb, but then again, I didn't feel the need to find out. I followed Josh's tracks and was at full throttle, yet Josh continued to pull away from me. It was obvious that it had become a race for him, and weighing in at about a hundred twenty five he was fifty pounds lighter. I had one advantage, and that was that he was forging the trail. I knew what was ahead, while he had no idea.

This reckless driving with no regards to safety couldn't help but make me think that this may have been the exact reason why he ended up in Rehab with me, but who was I trying to fool? I had the same type of "nothing can hurt me" mentality, but perhaps I had learned my lesson or maybe I was just a little older and wiser.

He continued to barrel ahead, never even slowing down at corners until finally, it happened. I had the good fortune of looking ahead, snowflakes blurring my vision as I watched him come to an abrupt halt, his wheelchair hanging precariously off a steep curb. His chair dipped forward, looking as if it was toppling over a cliff and then lurched to a stop. Josh's body flailed out then fell back as his seat belt tightened.

I assumed he would have been on his way by the time I reached the corner, but he was still there. His tires were suspended, spinning, and making contact with nothing but the air around them. I had to smile! What else could I do? What a precarious situation he found himself in. These chairs are rear wheel driven. His front wheel was safely on the road. His anti-tippers were squarely on the sidewalk and the wheels he needed to get around were in between.

I looked him in the eye with a smirk. He was laughing hysterically, his hands still pushing on the throttle. I truly believe he thought somehow this would dislodge him, but I had a different, more sensible answer. At least, I felt it more sensible. I backed my chair back twenty feet and headed towards the rear of his vehicle as fast as I dared. I made sure my tires were lined up to hit his and he moved a few inches. I went back and tried again, and this time his chair plunked down to the road Without the slightest "Thank You," he was off again. I did notice him slow down as he reached the other side of the street, though. I went back and took to the road.

My backtracking allowed Josh a good two-block lead and I was okay with that. He was willing to set the trail and I could safely follow along. It wasn't too long before Josh once again found himself in a similar predicament, but all the ramming in the world wasn't moving him an inch. It shouldn't have been funny. It was dark, except for the streetlights. It was snowing and we were alone, but we couldn't help but find the humor of the situation. Eventually, an older gentleman in a suit was nearby. He walked over and easily freed Josh's chair.

I'm sure he was more than a little taken aback by two quadriplegics in wheel-chairs laughing uncontrollably for being stuck on a cold winter night.

We were both careful not to let this happen again. We found ourselves checking for ramps at the end of each block and when there wasn't one, either crossing the street or taking to the road until we found a ramp back to the sidewalk.

Luckily the traffic was sparse, which was unusual for Chicago, and the streets were lit up well. We only had to do it a few times and usually just for a block. When you travel on sidewalks in a wheelchair you'll often find yourself at the end of a block with no ramp. It happens in small and large cities alike. It's a frustrating thing. You either need to know how to pop a wheelie with-out wheelie bars or back track and find a new way to get where your going, which often means going out onto the street. Obviously, this could be very dangerous. I always try to cross the street when possible, but that's not always an option either.

We arrived at Hooters much later then expected. A Hooters girl opened the door for us and we took our chairs inside, along with a ton of white and somewhat brownish snow. I felt bad making a mess of their floors, but what are you going to do? Our waitress led us to a table and we pulled in across from each other. I ordered hot wings and Josh ordered a hotdog. Eating the wings was a little difficult, but by using both my hands I got it done. Josh had his hotdog cut up by our waitress and the waitress helped him get his utensil holder on his finger. She then inserted his fork inside it. Josh was stoked and didn't stop talking. His eating had improved dramatically, and he was used to using gravity to take the place of not having triceps. He was on his last bite, and in mid conversation, when he became careless and some-how stabbed his cheek with his fork. I looked at him. A few small droplets of blood were finding their way out of his right cheek. I knew he wasn't hurt bad, and fighting back laughter, I told him he was bleeding. We once again found ourselves laughing. The waitress didn't seem to share in the humor of the situation and seemed quite concerned. She wet a napkin, wiped his cheek, and soon returned with a band-aid. I have a hunch she didn't understand why we were laughing, but if she had been living the lives we had, she might have. We were always laughing.

Maybe it was a coping mechanism. It was the people that hadn't been in contact with people in our situation that seemed most disturbed at our constant disregard for the seriousness of the situation. Maybe, it being their first encounter, they were still reeling with the catastrophic magnitude of our injuries. We, on the other hand, had already dealt with it in our own way. Heck! We live with it. It no longer bothered us like it used to. The effects of our accidents couldn't be changed, so what other choice is there than to make the most of it?

We headed back to RIC. The snow was continuing to fall and had gotten quite heavy. We were careful not to get caught up on any curbs, but the going was slow. Both of our batteries were almost out of bars. As RIC appeared a few blocks ahead, we held our fingers crossed that we would make it. Josh must have crossed his better than I crossed mine. Thirty feet from the front doors, my chair came to an abrupt stop. Josh went ahead and disappeared through the front doors. A few minutes later I was getting lectured on the dangers of our little exploit as attendants from RIC helped get me into a manual chair and pushed me inside the building.

Josh left on Monday morning. He was set up to live with his parents. His parents had come up a few times to learn how to take care of their son. They had remodeled their bathroom and built ramps so he could access the house. How sad that a split second can totally change not only one per-son's life, but all those around them as well.

I still had a week left before my insurance was up and my therapy would end. I was fortunate to have such good insurance. I had arrived earlier and left later than anyone else I knew.

I always felt I worked hard, but I worked especially hard that final week. Not just in therapy, but in the evenings as well. Friday I stayed up late just sitting in my chair thinking. I was in the room adjacent to where we always had our meals. It was the same room I had watched movies and attended informational seminars. It had a mat where I would sometimes transfer onto and work on moving my legs. There were soft rolls on the mat that I would place under my knees and straighten my legs. It was quiet with all the patients now in their room and probably asleep. I felt deep in my soul an acceptance; a feeling of contentment permeating throughout my mind and soul. I had worked hard throughout these months.

I had recovered more than most thought I would, and I knew it was just the beginning. I knew I had a long journey ahead of me, and that was okay.

The room had windows, but they were too high to see anything but the top of the skyscrapers that made up downtown Chicago. I wanted to look at the city. I wheeled my chair to a set of parallel bars situated near the wall. I pulled myself up to a standing position and gazed out onto the bustling city. I wonder if it's a similar feeling to what a person imprisoned feels when looking out of their cell window. A feeling of detachment, as if a whole other world is going on while you are trapped in your own. Honestly, I was afraid of going home the next day, but I was truly satisfied with what I had accomplished while I was here.

Gazing out the window at all the people walking along the sidewalk going in and out of businesses, I felt as though it was all on a screen and I was watching this at some theater. It was no longer my world. It made me afraid to think I would soon be a part of that world. My outlook on life was different. The things I valued had become more cerebral and less physical. I felt I was looking at the world the way it really is, and not the way we are groomed from birth to look at things. There is a spiritual awareness out there that many people are blinded to see. I no longer felt myself a slave to watching a clock and feeling the pressure to follow a time line. I no longer felt the quest to acquire material things. Money and everything associated with it can put you in a trance. You never know you're in the trance until you come out of it. It's much like falling in love with the wrong person. While you're in love, you don't see all the things that would normally tell you that it isn't right, but when you finally fall out of love, those same things seem obviously clear.

My mind pondered as I looked out that window that last night. It seemed as though I was looking at an ant farm down there on that sidewalk, with everyone on a mission to make their particular nest better.

It's easier to be paralyzed or physically handicapped when you value your mind. It is far more important than the ability to walk. I would never want to go through this again. I would love to just start walking across this tiled floor, but with the blinders taken off, a gift of insight was given to me. A gift that would become part of me and encompass my being for the rest of my life.

I woke up early and my nurse helped get me packed. I didn't have much to pack other than my clothes. Chelsea, Cindy and her mother arrived later that morning, packed up my belongings in the car and then came to get me. We took the elevator to the first floor and signed out for the last time. I wanted to prove something to myself, a commitment that this injury had not defeated me. I had Cindy give me my walker and I began walking toward the door. The guard came over when I was about halfway there and told me I wasn't allowed to use my walker until I was out of the building.

He said I needed to be taken out in my wheelchair, but I kept walking towards the door and the guard made no effort to stop me, each step becoming progressively more difficult. I felt a rush of emotion as I trudged through that exit door dragging my feet across the last few tiles of the rehab center, the brisk air rushing into my lungs. Gazing down the long sidewalks of Chicago I was filled with a sense of accomplishment. I collapsed into my wheelchair. Once again I had tears rolling down my cheeks.

I remember watching the Olympics as a kid and wondering why so many athletes break into tears after their events. I didn't quite understand, but now I do. It wasn't the event that brought them to tears, but the journey they had to take to make it there. The best part of reaching a goal isn't necessarily attaining it, but in the sacrifices you had to make to try. This was just something I needed to do for myself. I pushed my chair down the sidewalk and to the parking lot. I transferred into the front seat of the car. I was heading home, and this time for good.

Cindy had the basement all set up for me. There was a mattress on the floor with blankets. I also had numerous urine bottles that were given to us from the center. I smile when I say given, because I'm sure if I looked at my medical bill I paid for every one of them, and most likely, considerably more than they were worth.

I was suffering from a Urinary Tract Infection and was low on energy. I spent most of my first week in the basement recovering from the infection and popping my Amoxicillin along the way. Sleeping on the floor was not a good solution to my problem. It caused me to be dependent. Getting from the floor to my chair was still a monumental task. I had a box of catheters and a few tubes of lubricant and I found myself filling up all those urine bottles during the course of the day.

There were full urine bottles all around my makeshift bed. These bottles had to be emptied by Cindy. This situation left me feeling rather worthless and I'm sure it wasn't ideal for Cindy as well. This was a situation that needed to change as soon as possible.

Soft mattresses were like quicksand to me, and the bed we had in the bedroom was even worse; it was a waterbed. A water mattress for a person in my condition is equivalent to a fly on flypaper. Or better yet, a fish floundering after washing up on the beach. Getting into the waterbed was nearly impossible and once I landed on the mattress I was destined to stay in whatever that position happened to be when I came to rest. Newton's Law states that an object at rest will stay at rest until some force acts upon it, and that force was someone helping me.

Once on the bed I would even feel a sense of panic. You have probably already figured out that I don't like to feel trapped, and that waterbed made me feel the same way I did those first few weeks after my accident. I think I speak for quite a few people when I say it's a terrible feeling being unable to move. It's a form of claustrophobia that I just couldn't endure, so it was evident that this bed just wasn't going to work for me.

Cindy and I went together to a local bedding store and bought a new bed. We settled on a King size mattress that was extra firm. The firmer the mattress, the easier it was for me to move. We bought flannel sheets, which turned into a nightmare because people with limited mobility will tend to scoot and slide themselves around. Sliding and scooting across flannel creates a lot of friction, and eventually I had rug burns all over my elbows and knees. We then tried satin sheets, which took the problem to the complete opposite end of the spectrum. Now It was like a deer on a frozen pond, or like my Lab puppy was whenever the tiled floor in the kitchen was waxed; legs flying in every direction trying to get a foothold. I remember how much fun it was to call her and watch her back legs spinning as she tried to run around the kitchen table, sometimes sliding into the cupboards.

I finally settled in on just plain cotton sheets, and they seemed to work the best. They had enough friction to get a foothold, but not so much that I was burning my skin. A big part of succeeding is creating a situation that promotes success.

I now could start sleeping in my own bed, transferring to my chair, and gaining some much needed independence. I think of people like Tim who relied on others for each and every thing and wonder how I would have coped. It would have been really hard. People mention how happy I always am, but without independence I'm not so sure that would be the case. I can never overstate just how important it is to be able to do things on your own. Just another reminder that there are many people worse off than me and to be thankful and grateful for all I have.

I spent the coming weeks getting used to my new surroundings and new routines. My Mother-In-Law was taking care of Chelsea each day, but in time I was able to take care of her too. It was a bit surreal taking care of another human being when it had been me that needed to be taken care of for so long. It was wonderful to get to spend so much time with my daughter each day. I truly missed her those days when she went to stay with her grandmother. The accident had drawn Chelsea and her grandparents very close. I knew they were going to miss having her all day, but I couldn't have been happier spending time with her.

Chelsea was two and a half years old and a very compassionate soul. She would notice my difficulties in doing things. I had hoped she would remember what I was like before the accident, but she had few memories from back then. One day, when I was struggling to get up into my walker from the bed she said to me "Daddy, it's like this," and walked across the room. She was trying to teach me to walk. I smiled and commented on how well she was able to walk. It wasn't all that long ago, before my accident, that I was watching her pull herself up to her feet and take a few steps before tumbling back down. Each day I watched her make it a few more steps until finally walking across the room on two feet. It's ironic how life can sometimes go full circle.

CHAPTER FOURTEEN
The Assembly

I had another month before my return to the tennis courts to coach the River King tennis team. The school had contacted me that they were having an assembly of the student body and they wanted me to come and speak.

The gymnasium was packed with students. I was excited to be in front of the entire student body, which amounted to more than a thousand students. The students were equally excited, most likely at the prospect of missing class. The Principal went to the microphone to talk a little about my accident and current situation.

The room was buzzing with the chatter of students. I sat in my wheelchair in the corner, kind of in the wings, out of sight from most of the student body. Cindy was standing next to me with walker in hand as the Principal was addressing the students. He said, "As you know, we have been trying to raise money for tennis coach David Moore these past few weeks after his Spinal Cord Injury, and it has been extremely successful. You have been competing to see which class would receive the most votes. A penny in your class's container was worth a vote, but a dollar bill was worth negative one hundred votes. The class with the most votes will get to decide which of the four teacher volunteers will get their head shaved. But before we give you the results, we would like to invite David Moore to come up and say a few words."

I was maybe fifty feet from the podium. I rolled my chair to within twenty feet before I took the walker from Cindy and walked the rest of the way. The moment my body raised up from that chair a loud noise broke out in the room. I could see all the students in the stands, on their feet, cheering and clapping. The sound was deafening and it continued the entire way to the stand. I took hold of the podium and looked all around me. More than a thousand students and faculty were on their feet.

I stood for what seemed like hours, but was closer to a minute. It seemed like an eternity standing there listening to the applause. I felt a rush of emotion encapsulate my entire body. I felt my eyes blur and begin to water. When the applause finally died down I began to speak, but had trouble making out words. My throat quivered as I tried to hold back tears. I continued trying to speak clearly and as I spoke my voice eventually became clearer and clearer.

"I want to thank everyone for thinking of me and my family. It is incredible that you have taken the time to have a fundraiser in my honor. I have been in the hospital and in therapy for quite awhile and have made many improvements." I looked up at students in the stands and it was eerily silent. The chatter was replaced with their undivided attention. Perhaps their attention was similar to the attention I had so long ago watching the "Other Side of the Mountain." The realization of how fragile life is and how easily my situation could be their own. Regardless of what was going through their minds, they had chosen to stop and listen to every word I had to say. I wish I could tell you exactly what I said, but it wasn't a speech I wrote down. I had no idea what was coming out of my mouth until I said it. It was a speech of gratitude for all the kindness that had been showered upon me by so many people. When I finished, the students stood again and cheered as I made my way back to my chair.

I sat in my wheelchair as the assembly continued. The speaker announced that the Senior Class had gotten the most votes. The Senior Class, by virtue of having the most votes, got to choose which of the four teachers would get their head shaven.

They picked one of the most popular teachers in the school. This teacher was a man who always had a smile on his face. He always had positive things to say, and would help anyone he could. He was now going to have his full head of hair shaved down to his scalp for the sake of a fundraiser to help my family and I. The president of the Senior Class came out of the stands. She was handed the electric clippers, and to the delight of the entire student body, ran it across the middle of his head, front to back. The crowd erupted as a ball of hair fell to the floor next to him and a reverse Mohawk lined the center of his head.

I left the gymnasium that day with my heart overflowing with warmth, a calmness gently washing over me and lodging deep into my soul. Compassion from others has a healing effect that is hard to explain. I felt absolutely at ease that day. I felt I could conquer anything.

HIGH SCHOOLS
Road to Recovery
coach Dave Moore returns to the tennis court

...nton boys tennis coach Dave Moore keeps an eye on his troops.

Mark Hagen/QUAD-CITY TIMES

I couldn't feel hot or cold be... there were no nerve endings the top of my skin. My hands ...n't working, and I had to be by someone," he said, flashing a ...le as he polished off eating a ...l of cereal.

"I was in physical rehab in Dav... ...rt for about five hours a day, ... would get tired very quickly, discouraging part was that after ...or six weeks, I was only able to ...e my knees about an inch."

...t was then determined Moore

couragement, with people praying for me to keep battling. Deep down, I always had a sense that things eventually would be OK."

After about two months and eight or nine hours of therapy every day, he was able to lift his knee six inches. It led to movement in his ankles and toes, and soon his stom... ...ach muscles began to gain some strength.

"By the time I left Chicago in mid-January, after being there about four months, I was able to

his junior high basketball coaching position at Clinton's Washington Middle School, he was determined he would coach the Clinton tennis team this spring.

"All through this, all the kids I come in contact with were great in sending me letters encouraging me," Moore said. "Sometimes you don't realize what a big effect you have on student-athletes until something like this happens."

Obviously, he still has a long way to go.

step on my own, and eventually walk again," he said. "In my mind, the only thing I may never do again is run, and I'm not saying that will never happen."

Who can say he won't soon be doing all those things.

Moore was done talking about himself and his amazing recovery. He wanted to visit about his tennis team.

"We have 33 kids out this spring, ...

It was early March, and although still quite chilly, I had my first tennis practice since my accident. I had grown accustomed to talking in front of people, but it was different that first day speaking to the kids. Perhaps it was the fact that I always associated sports with being able bodied. I may have had more doubts than the kids that day. I still wondered if I was going to be a good coach, but I got the feeling the kids weren't as pessimistic. I remember them seemingly listening even more intently to what I had to say than before my spinal cord injury. I prepared myself in the hospital for this day. The day when someone might question my authority, but nothing like that ever materialized. That first day and every day after was spent much like before my accident. I couldn't demonstrate like before, but I replaced that by detailing things a bit more vividly through communication. I explained what I wanted from them and when needed I had some of my more advanced players demonstrate the shots and techniques I was trying to instill in them. Practices went better and smoother than I had ever expected.

We were a week from our first match when I received a phone call from a local TV station. They wanted to do a short story centered on my return to coaching. The reporter showed up at practice the following day with cameras in tow. They interviewed me as well as some of my players and Cindy. I watched the piece that night on the news. It lasted a few minutes. It made me feel good to hear my players make positive comments on my return. The reporter asked them if I was any different than before my injury. They said "No," and they too mentioned that I just had to explain things better than before. It was just a short piece, but must have been noticed by the two other major stations. I found myself on all three TV stations in the course of a week, each one putting their own slant on my story. Maybe it's best I keep quiet, but I felt somewhat like the latest story, like the stations didn't want to be outdone by one another. Regardless of intent, the stories were heartfelt, and no doubt touched some viewers in a positive way. I had become quite the softie and it didn't take much to make my eyes moisten up. Hearing my story through other people's eyes just gave it a sense of reality that I couldn't have internalized by myself.

It was the day before our first meet when my brand new "Tennis Wheelchair" arrived. My current chair was heavy and hard to push, but my new chair was half the weight. The new chair had wheels that cambered out to the side and only one front wheel for quick maneuverability. It was made to play tennis in and was so much quicker than my previous chair. I couldn't wait to get into it and tool around. It took a bit of getting used to as I only had to lean back slightly and the chair would rise up into a wheelie. I was looking forward to taking my new chair to my match the following day.

It was a beautiful sunny afternoon. The team bus sat in the back of the lot and soon was filled with the hustle and bustle of twenty-five tennis players looking forward to their first match. I showed a couple of seniors how to remove the wheels to my chair and then stood in front of the bus door holding onto the rail. I found places to grab and eventually pulled myself into the bus.

I make a habit of using upper body strength to compensate for the weakness in my legs. There is usually an answer to most problems. There were so many tasks I thought I couldn't do only to find ways to overcome them. It usually comes down to a combination of patience and perseverance. I eventually found myself falling into the front seat as players loaded my wheelchair in the seat across from me. Thirty minutes later we were pulling into North High School and I was guiding the driver to the back of the building where the tennis courts were. I told the kids to put all their equipment in the same spot and to head out onto the courts to warm up.

I was the last to get off the bus, my chair sitting next to the bus door thanks to my helpful seniors. Sitting in my chair, a steep, grassy hill stood between the tennis courts and myself. The players were all lumbering down the luscious spring grass heading towards the courts, but I was now presented with a problem: how to get down this hill?

I began searching for a sidewalk, and soon found one just a few hundred feet away. I remember that beautiful day as I looked down on this concrete sidewalk making a beeline down this steep hill. I sat there in my new sports chair and a smile came to my face. I hadn't had a chance to really test my new chair yet and what a wonderful opportunity this seemed to be. I figured I would head down this sidewalk and let my chair pick up a little speed before using my hands to slow down. I pushed my chair to the edge of the precipice and over it. My chair sped up much quicker than I expected and within moments I was flying. A feeling of panic swept over me as I grabbed my push rims to slow down. They had a rubber coating to maximize their grip. I felt the burning pain as the rims burned right into the skin. I grabbed them again but it was destroying my hands, it was like putting my hands against a sander. My palms were already bleeding. I couldn't slow down. There was nothing I could do. I relented to my fate and flew down the hill, hands at my side. I didn't dare touch the rims again. It wouldn't have done any good if I had. My chair continued to pick up speed, and I had a look of terror as my chair went faster and faster until I reach the turn that took me to the tennis courts. It was a ninety-degree turn but I flew past it in a straight line doing what I can only guess was over twenty miles per hour.

My chair flew off the sidewalk and headed towards the football field. No sooner had my chair left the concrete than my small front wheel dug deep into the soft spring soil. The chair came to a sudden and abrupt stop. My chair stopped instantly, but unfortunately I did not. I was flying superman style towards the end zone, my face skidding across the wet grass until finally coming to a sliding stop.

My face was still buried in a combination of wet grass and mud when I heard voices yell down to me. "Are you all right? Are you all right"? I said, "Yes," as I felt both of my arms being grabbed. As I was pulled up, I looked to see the two men who were lifting me. They both were wearing officiating uniforms. They were able to get me back into my wheelchair as I looked up to see two soccer teams gathered just a few feet from me, all staring. I glanced over to the stadium only to see a few hundred soccer fans doing the same. I had flown into and disrupted a high school soccer game.

Feeling embarrassed would be a bit of an understatement as I headed down the sidewalk towards my team. I was fortunate that a large maintenance garage blocked the view from the courts. I pulled up to the team and a few players asked why my clothes were covered in grass stains, but I acted like I hadn't heard it, and began talking about our upcoming match. It would be years before I told any of them what happened that day. I learned the importance of wearing gloves to avoid going down hills out of control. This would never happen again. I do dumb things, but rarely do them more than once, "okay, maybe sometimes!"

My first season went along well coaching from a wheelchair. It taught me to explain better than I had before, to use veteran players for examples when I wanted to demonstrate a lesson, and most of all, it taught me to communicate better. We finished third out of ten teams that year. It just so happened that we were also hosting the conference tournament and as the head coach of the hosting school I was in charge of the coaches meeting.

I mention what happened, not because it was directly related to my spinal cord injury, but because all actions, all interactions, and all of life in general overlap with each other. One affects the other, regardless of their size or scope. Our environment has a constant influence on our lives.

I was sitting in my wheelchair in front of nine other head coaches and their assistants going over the rules, court assignments and such things that would enable the upcoming tournament to go smoothly. I was in the midst of my speech when my wife Cindy came into the room. She walked up and whispered in my ear, "Your father passed away." It's one of those moments that you never forget. It stays with you for the rest of your life.

I had talked to my father just the day before on the phone. I told him I had to run this tournament, but that the following day I planned on coming to visit him. It's a decision I regret to this very day. I should have visited him that day. I had nothing I couldn't have put off, but I believed there would be a tomorrow. I left for the hospital to find him dead in his bed with a painful expression across his face. He had been fighting cancer and had seemed to be doing better when he suffered a massive heart attack.

We never know when our final day will be, but I know not to take life for granted. Make an effort to find the time to stop and talk. Always be kind and exude a positive spirit towards others. We never know if we'll ever get another chance.

I couldn't stop shaking in my hospital bed the days following my accident. I knew that it could have been my final day. I always thought there would be a tomorrow for my father and I would visit him, but tomorrow doesn't always come. Appreciate life and the lives of others while you can. It can end in a moment and there's no going back. I wish I would have visited him the day before the tournament rather than the day after, but I guess these things happen in life to help us learn a lesson. I now think the most tragic thing is to be given a life lesson and fail to learn from it. Live every day like it's your last, and treat all those around you as if you may never see them again. I say "I love you" so many more times now then I ever did before.

I don't remember how the team did in that tournament. I didn't really care then, and I still don't. I think that my experience brought an awareness of how insignificant the sports themselves are. The discipline, learning to work with others, striving to be better than you were, are all wonderful side effects and all part of the journey. There's a place for watching sports, but it ranks near the bottom when it comes to living life. I've learned that the importance of the journey far outweighs the destination. The journey is life, the destination but a point in time.

I was once a sports watching junkie and I still enjoy watching sports, but find it almost comical when people take it to such an extreme that they let it encompass their whole being. I once dated a girl who was a rabid Green Bay Packers fan and we broke up because I wasn't one. Funny how sometimes blessings are disguised as setbacks. "Be moderate in all things" is a wonderful lesson. When kids I'm teaching are struggling, I always tell them to remember it's just a game. The important thing is preparing and giving your best. If you do that, then winning or losing isn't an issue.

You can only control yourself and what you do or don't do, but you can't control what others do. Sometimes your opponent is just better than you that day.

I still had my dream of walking normally again. I used my walker everywhere. I couldn't grocery shop with my walker, but I did use it to walk from the parking lot to the door and then use their motorized cart. I used it to get gas. I used it at the house. I wanted to be like I was, but I ignored the fact that I wasn't the same person I used to be.

I have a feeling that anyone reading this that hasn't had a spinal cord injury or is still in the early stages of their injury may not understand, but I will explain it as best I can. I spent years refusing to use my wheelchair unless absolutely necessary. I struggled every time I used my walker. I couldn't get anywhere fast. To tell you the truth, I got there very, very slowly. I couldn't carry anything while using my walker and I could only go a very short distance before I had to stop. I would need to find a place to sit before I could go any further, and my entire life during those years was so limited. I didn't enjoy the things I otherwise could have because I was stubborn and put a heavy emphasis on walking as making me whole.

I speak for myself, but I know others who have come to the same conclusion. Just like so many years before when I watched Jill Kinmont confined to a wheelchair and thinking how horrible it would be to no longer be able to run or walk and not knowing if I'd ever want to live like that. In time there comes a realization, and that realization is that there is so much more to life than being able to walk. I have often said that when my lower body was taken away, I became better above my shoulders. When something's taken away, something else grows stronger.

I can't sit here and honestly say I don't want to run or walk or play sports again, because I do. I can say that I accept my situation without resigning myself to it. I can say that enjoying life on two feet or two wheels is still enjoying life.

CHAPTER FIFTEEN
The Real World

It really did seem that life outside the hospital was a bit like a prisoner being released from jail. I have to admit I'm basing this mostly on what I've seen in movies. When prisoners were released in the movie "Shawshank Redemption," they seemed out of their element. The structure of everyday life was absent. Uncertainty of what the future might hold was painfully evident. Some prisoners even ended their life or committed crimes just to get back to where they felt comfortable.

On the one hand it sounds crazy to prefer incarceration over freedom, but on the other hand, there's a lot to be said for knowing what lies ahead of you each day. I felt that uneasiness in what I like to refer to as "the real world". Each day was now different than the one before. It seemed the need for survival was heightened, that somehow I needed to compete with those around me. I had spent almost the entire time since my accident in a positive mindset, with only a couple of exceptions, and now I was struggling to stay positive.

The high school season was over, and now it was time to teach summer tennis lessons. I had been teaching summer tennis lessons since I was eighteen. I had taught in Clinton, IA, for the past five years. Summer lessons were going to be different than coaching. The pupils I would be teaching would range from four to eighteen years in age, and in the evening I had adult lessons. Back when I was in the hospital, I would often lie on my back and think about summer tennis lessons. I had so much time to think back then. I wondered how the young kids would accept me.

The first day of lessons started on a brisk, sunny morning. Each lesson was an hour long with the youngest students starting out in the morning. Each successive hour would see the kids gradually get older, and in the afternoon, the high school kids would be rolling in.

I sat in my wheelchair that first morning looking out at the courts. In years past I would be out throwing balls to kids by now, but today I was off to the side just waiting for the first lesson to begin. There were about thirty kids in the class ranging from four to seven. I recognized about half of them from the previous year. It wasn't like me to lack in confidence, but I felt very insecure that morning. I rolled out onto the courts as the kids sat down for our opening day talk. Cindy, who taught lessons with me, began going over all the rules, like what to do if it's raining, bring water, etc.

She introduced the instructors, saving me for last. When she said my name, the children gazed in my direction. Perhaps it was because of where my mind was at that moment, but it seemed they looked in my direction longer than in years past. So much of how we are perceived by others is how we project ourselves from inside. If the kids looked at me longer than normal it was probably due to my own insecurities.

We divided the kids into groups. The children who knew me from years past seemed to treat me just as they always did. There were only a handful of kids who seemed afraid or perhaps wary of coming too close. It helped me to be teaching tennis because this was my element and an environment I felt comfortable with. As each day passed, my confidence grew, and the kids' confidence in me grew as well. After a few days the kids would huddle closely around my chair as I talked to them. It was almost an advantage to talk to them at eye level. I always had their undivided attention, even more than when I was able bodied.

This experience made me appreciate children even more. They embraced my condition better than even adults. Children are born free from racism, prejudice and all the horrible afflictions of thought we can sometimes acquire when we grow older. I couldn't help but think that their experience with someone in a wheelchair might carryover to their adulthood, and they might be better able to embrace others who may not be exactly like themselves. I would like to think I had a positive influence that would affect them throughout their lives. This was the deal I made with a higher being while I lay paralyzed in my hospital bed so many months ago; I needed to get better to make a positive influence on others.

I had hand controls installed on Cindy's old car. It was large enough to hold my wheelchair if the wheels were removed, and they were easily taken off with just a push of a button. I was walking with my walker whenever possible. I would walk as far as I could until I became so tired I was unable to lift my legs anymore. I would then drag them along the ground. I walked so much like this that after the summer I wore holes into the front part of my shoes.

I felt I could conquer my ambulatory problem by walking at every possible moment. I could strengthen my legs, and everything would be just as it had been before the accident. I had to think when I walked. Lift the knee, straighten the leg, lean forward, lift the other knee, etc. I walked slowly and cerebral. I had plenty of experience working out while able bodied, but this was much harder for me. The thinking part is what made it so hard. I had to concentrate on every little movement, and then when I did move my legs, it felt as though they weighed hundreds of pounds.

At the end of the summer my walking had improved quite a bit, but I really didn't notice it like I should have. I thought I'd be farther along. My legs were still heavy and my endurance weak, but in contrast from where it had been, I had made great strides (forgive the pun!). I had a friend who had seen me walking throughout the summer and told me I was going to walk normally again. He said if I could take one step, I can take two, then four, and eventually be walking wherever I wanted. I knew he didn't understand. I'm sure that statement seems to make sense, but I knew the only thing that really seemed to improve that summer was my conditioning. Important things like balance and control were still poor, and my strength was nowhere near what it needed to be to walk without my walker. Yet, as I've said before, it's the journey and not the destination. It's the belief that I will be better tomorrow than I am today.

I was given a cheap wheelchair from a friend, which I kept in the house. My tennis chair was kept in the trunk of my car. I only had one cushion, so it stayed with the chair in the house. My tennis chair had two rows of Velcro on the seat. It was there to adhere the cushion, but since I didn't have one, I used a towel folded over. Cushions cost hundreds of dollars, and it was my intent to buy one, but I kept putting it off.

My spasms began getting worse and worse to the point that I would sometimes collapse while trying to walk with my walker. I mentioned to Cindy the pain that was seemingly coming from my knee. She was leaning over my legs looking at my knees when she mentioned a disgusting smell. She had me pull myself up into standing position with my walker and looked at the back of my legs.

A shiver went flashing through my spine as Cindy let out a shriek. "Oh David! What did you do to the back of your leg?" I replied, saying "I don't know what you're talking about." She said she wanted to puke, which is not the most encouraging comment to tell someone who's wondering what horrible thing has just befallen them. She continued saying that I had a large sore, practically to the bone, with puss oozing out of it. The sore was on the back of my thigh. I had known something wasn't quite right with my leg, but was surprised I couldn't feel something this massive.

It didn't take long to determine what the cause had been. The towel I was using only covered a portion of the velcro. Some velcro towards the front of my seat was uncovered. Each time I slid in and out of my seat I would rub the back of my leg across the strip until I had created a hole in the back of my leg. My leg had become infected, and was now oozing puss. I reached back and felt the wetness. I looked at my hand, covered in puss, and then I wanted to throw up. I never took a mirror to look at it. I just took antibiotics and kept it clean and treated. I stayed off it the best I could while it eventually healed.

I now know to wear gloves when taking a wheelchair down a hill and to always use a good cushion when sitting in my chair. I also know how important it is to check your body for sores on a regular basis. Sores not only set back your training, but can become septic and kill you. It's one of the major causes of death in severe spinal cord patients. This was a normal sore that had turned into a pressure sore. Many pressure sores start with a break in the skin just like this, and when untreated, they continue to grow until they become life threatening.

I was taking rehab treatments from the local hospital twice a week. I think my therapist was happy to work with me to see just how far I was capable of going. She was about five foot seven, pasty white skin, and dark brown hair. She was ultra health conscious. Her name was Callie.

I was there on numerous occasions when she had lunch. Lunch for her consisted of a bottle of water and a small handful of nuts, I even saw her eat just saltine crackers one time. Not really my idea of healthy, but it seemed to work for her.

She always seemed to have energy, though I'm not sure where she got it. It was definitely not from her diet. We worked on many things, but her main concern was with the quality of my gait. I still dragged my feet when I walked, especially once I tired, so she had me spend much of my time lifting my knees. I improved the quality of my walk with Callie, but once I was fatigued there wasn't much I could do but use the strength of my arms against the walker to drag each foot through. I was the only spinal cord patient at the hospital. I was probably the youngest also. Most of the patients in treatment were stroke victims. I've seen plenty of stroke victims since entering rehab and some make a full recovery, but most make a partial one. I have an immense amount of respect for Physical and Occupational Therapists. I never did come across a single one that didn't go above and beyond to help me reach my goals. It's more a way of life for them than a job. I can't tell you enough how much I respect and endear these people.

It was October, and the brisk air of impending winter was blowing in. My tennis lessons were over and I had a break in my therapies. Cindy, Chelsea, and myself decided to travel to Indiana and give Tim a visit.

Tim lived on this extensive farm in Midwestern Indiana. We passed through vast rows of golden brown corn just about ready for harvesting when we finally reached a large, rustic farmhouse. We pulled up and were instantly greeted by a trio of large dogs. They all looked to be mutts, of what origin, I couldn't even guess. I was just happy they were friendly as their tails wagged wildly upon our arrival. Tim was on his porch with that infectious grin looking down at us. He was still in that same behemoth of a chair I was so accustomed to.

I knew it was going to be easy for me to visit Tim. Many times going to someone else's house is a real struggle to get around, but Tim had his entire house renovated with ramps. The doors were widened. His bathroom had a roll in shower. He had access to every area of his house.

Cindy retrieved my chair from the trunk as I waited in the passenger seat. I transferred quickly to my chair and headed up the ramp to the porch. I reached out to Tim and put my hand on his, which was spread out flat on his hand rest. I knew he couldn't feel it, but it was a symbolic gesture of friendship. We had a special bond, having gone through all this together. I often wonder if it's the same kind of bond I hear war veterans talk about.

We went inside where his brother and sister in law were seated. Tim's wife came in and gave me a hug. We spent the night having a couple of beers and playing cards. Tim's brother helped him, and I was able to play my own thanks to all that card manipulation I did back in the hospital.

The next morning was glorious, the sun was shining through the huge picture window and the smell of honey bacon was wafting from the stove. Breakfast on the farm is like no other. It's a wonder every farmer doesn't weigh a thousand pounds. Eggs, hash browns, honey bacon, ham, and an assortment of pastries, not to mention fresh orange juice and milk. I ate far more than I should have, but without regrets. I watched as Tim's wife fed him. Tim ate every bit as much as me, perhaps a little bit more.

I was always impressed with the loving and caring nature of his wife. The way she'd spoon food into his mouth and occasionally wipe his chin, all the while appearing to enjoy every second of it. It had to be a strain, but she never showed it. She was truly Tim's angel. When Tim had finished eating, she made a small plate for herself. There was a beauty and a sadness watching this all unfold. I wish I could just turn back the clock, but I can't. Tim didn't deserve this and his wife didn't either.

We followed Tim's van in our car. We took a tour of Tim's farm. He had leased his land out to some other farmers since he could no longer farm it himself, but it was still his and he was proud of it. He had cornfields, some soybeans, and a few pigs. I remember looking at his large barn and the towering silo alongside it, wondering if that's where his life had changed forever. I didn't have the fortitude to ask!

Later in the day it was time for us to go. Tim wheeled with me out to the car. There was no pavement; just hard, packed dirt. I said goodbye to Tim and his family and was ready to roll my chair over to the car. Tim's wife had said she heard I could walk with a walker, and asked me if I would show her. Cindy got my walker from the car and brought it to me.

I pulled myself up and walked to the car twenty or so feet away, then turned to face Tim and his family. Tim was happy for me, but in his face I saw extreme sadness as well. I always felt guilty walking around Tim. I purposely left my walker in the car on this trip for that very reason. The pain in his face behind that monstrous smile broke my heart. I knew what he was thinking. "Why can't I get along as well as him?" It really puts life into perspective. We all have our problems in varying degrees, and when you realize you're not alone, it makes it easier to deal with them. I don't think I could ever trade places with Tim, but if I had the chance, I'd have healed him instead of myself. I would do that without thinking twice. As each year passed I saw incremental improvements. I had acupuncture done, which improved my hand function slightly. My blood pressure and endurance got better. My insistence on using a walker every possible moment put a significant hindrance on my quality of life. I was limited on the distance I could walk and it took much longer. I also couldn't carry things while using my walker. A good example was when I went grocery shopping one afternoon.

I was in my car. The wheelchair was in the trunk, but the wheels were off and I wasn't able to put it together on my own. I didn't need to anyway because I had shopped at Eagles Supermarket many times. I would park in the handicap spot and take my walker to the front door, transfer onto their electric cart, and do my shopping. I would then drive the electric cart back to my car and load it. I had done it many times.

I parked my car and began traversing the lot with my walker. It was slow going; one incredibly slow step after another. I had about fifty feet to the door and had traveled about halfway when I saw a car pull into the lot. A heavyset man jumped out of his car and looked in my direction. Then he broke into a run. I was about ten feet from the door when he rushed passed me. I had a sense of what he was doing. This didn't appear to be someone who ran often. I watched as the door opened. My suspicions were confirmed when he jumped into the only electric cart and whisked off. Making it this far was about all I had in the tank. I turned and walked back to my car dragging both of my feet the entire way until collapsing into my front seat. I came back another time and did my shopping.

I was caught up with this notion that walking is what defined me. Somehow walking in a walker made me more whole than pushing a wheelchair. I know I'm not alone with this notion, but most people in similar conditions as mine realize that walking is not everything. I'm not saying walking isn't important, but it pales when compared to the ability to do things on your own. It took me years to figure out that I'd rather wheel into the kitchen, make myself breakfast, and eat it in the living room. I'd rather pick my daughter up from school and have her sit on my lap as I gave her a ride home. These and many other things aren't possible when using a walker. I found myself using my wheelchair more and more. Eventually I acquired a van, and didn't have to take apart and put back together my chair every time I used it. A whole new world of independence was laid out before me. I became far closer to what you might consider "normal". I still worked on my walking, but by using my wheelchair I could do everything on my own without the help of anyone else, and that was far more important than whether I was upright.

When my daughter was five, Cindy and I divorced. The injury may have played a part, but I think it was inevitable that this was going to happen. I was ready to live completely on my own. I had improved in small increments each and every year. The hardest part was seeing my young daughter cry, but over time it proved to be the best for everyone.

David and Chelsea

One year my friend Mark, who used to play catch with me in the hospital, asked if I'd like to go to New York City and spend time in Manhattan. We decided on spending about ten days there and also visit the US Tennis Tournament.

Mark was an athlete all his life and he liked to walk everywhere he went. We rarely ever used a taxi, and only used the subway when it was a long distance. Most days we were exploring the streets of Manhattan with him walking and me rolling. I would push my chair for hours and after a couple of days, my hands were riddled with blisters. Mark, being the amazing friend he is, slipped out early one morning, found a bike shop, and brought me a pair of gloves for the rest of the trip. Another valuable lesson: it's important to wear gloves when pushing your chair long distances. The ten days went quickly and soon we were at La Guardia airport for the return trip home.

We encountered a major problem while at La Guardia. We needed to get to the upper floor to catch our gate, but the elevators were down. We didn't have much time, so I told Mark I had done the escalators in Chicago. I just needed him to follow right behind and help if needed. The place was buzzing with people and a seemingly endless stream of people were boarding and exiting the moving stairs.

I would be a lie if I said I wasn't afraid. I remember using the escalator back in Chicago, and it wasn't easy even with all those people helping. However, my arms were much stronger now. I would never try this unless it was absolutely necessary, and it seemed I had little other choice.

I knew I had to go in backwards. Going in forward would cause my chair to flip over and with the stairs in constant motion may have caused some major carnage. I backed my chair up to the escalator and eased my way on. I held tight to the moving rails on both sides of me. The metal below quickly changed into stairs and my chair violently lurched forward. I held on with all my might. My wheelchair was pointing nearly straight down with my front wheel settling on the stair below. Without the rails to hold onto, I would have rolled right out of my chair with my chair tumbling behind me. Everything seemed to be going great. Mark was right in front of me, and right behind him was an escalator packed with people. All I had to do is hold on until I reached the top.

You have to understand that during this entire process I was riddled with fear and holding on with everything I had. I knew I was only one mistake from what could be a painful accident. Finally, we reached the top. That's when I choked. When the wheels of my chair reached that stationary metal strip that marked the end of the ride I continued to hold onto the rail. In a split second my chair flipped over and I was lying on my back atop the escalator with my front wheel pointing skyward.

I heard a loud commotion going on, but I couldn't see it. I was stuck on my back facing the ceiling of the airport. I was trying to get my chair to move, but was basically immobile. Luckily, there were two airport attendants nearby, and I was pulled out in about fifteen seconds. I knew what had happened to me, but was completely unaware of the panic I had caused.

Mark walked over to me, clearly shook up, and began explaining what had occurred during those fifteen seconds. My chair has two large back wheels and one small one in front. The front wheel extends out from the chair about a foot or so. Mark had been hovering over my chair in case I needed help. When my chair flipped, the small front wheel that extends out flew quickly up Mark's leg and underneath his shorts.

There was real fear in his face when he said that he thought he might be castrated right then and there. He said he couldn't get the wheel out from under his shorts, and all the while, people were backed up behind him all scrambling to walk backward down the escalator so they wouldn't crash into both of us. I have a feeling some harsh words were said about me that day and probably deservedly so, but then again, how can the elevators be down at the airport?

Each year that passed found my condition improving ever so slightly. It wasn't necessarily with walking, but things like breathing. I couldn't yell, and had trouble singing. I had to take short breaks when talking to catch my breath, but now my breathing had gotten stronger and with it my endurance. My ability to urinate had steadily improved. It used to take fifteen minutes to urinate and now it was down to five or less. I knew exactly where to push my stomach to induce this to happen. I ate better and understood my body well enough that I could manage my bowels. I ate more vegetables and took a pro-biotic each day. I only moved my bowels once or twice a week, but that worked for me.

I had dated off and on over the years and one day I met a young lady named Julie. I think you'd be hard pressed to find anyone who didn't like Julie. She had this glow about her, always beaming with a huge smile and never having anything but positive things to say. She had short brown hair that curled slightly at her shoulders. She was about five foot six and looked very healthy.

Julie was very active, enjoyed swimming everyday, and when possible she'd go for a run. She enjoyed cooking, and often made healthy dishes like stir-fry or grilled chicken. It seemed everything she made not only tasted great, but was also good for you. She did introduce me to Haagen Dazs ice cream, but other than that, I was eating better than ever.

I was still active, but my regiment had slowed since those early days. Julie would change all that. She wanted me to go with her on a run one sunny day. It was late spring, and we drove out to a bike trail. I put my gloves on and she her running shoes. She ran with me at first, but upon my urging, she took off on her own pace. I tried with all my might to keep up, but she was too fast for me. I watched as she got smaller and smaller in the distance.

She stopped after a couple of miles and waited for me. I was exhausted by the time I got there. Little did I know at the time that she had just gotten me started on my new passion of pushing my wheelchair long distances.

Julie and I went out that whole summer. I learned through experimentation how to go faster and faster. Trying to grip the push rims slowed me down. It would slow you down even with good hands. My hands were still severely impaired, but making contact with the palm and using friction to slap the hand forward allowed a much faster ride. I got to the point that I could keep up with Julie on most days and what used to be two miles became five and sometimes more.

This exercise strengthened my arms and the rest of my body like nothing else had. I found myself going out on my own whenever Julie couldn't, sometimes pushing my chair ten miles or more. I found a cemetery near my house that was built on a hill where I could really test myself. Thirty minutes of hills were harder for me than hours of flat ground. I entered my first race since I got hurt that year. Julie and I signed up for a half marathon. We did just over thirteen miles with Julie helping push me up the major hills. I felt a little bit like I did before the accident. I always enjoyed sports and that sense of accomplishing your goals.

The following year saw me heading out nearly everyday. I pushed my chair wherever I could and always found time for the hills. There were two hills in the cemetery I had trouble with. I always had to stop halfway up to let my arms rest, but as my strength continued to improve I found myself making it all the way up without stopping. Eventually, I never had to stop at all. I told myself at that point to never stop on a hill. To push, regardless of how slow, until you reached the top. A big part to anything you do in life involves telling yourself you can do it.

I remember giving a talk to my tennis team on that exact subject. I normally tried not to integrate my injury into our talks, but on this day I told them how many times I had fallen when trying to walk. There was rarely a time I didn't have scabs on either my elbows or my knees, but I found the secret that kept me from falling. I fell when I let negative thoughts enter my brain. It was then that my legs would buckle and I'd fall to the ground, so I never let negative thoughts enter my mind.

I would pull myself up from my walker telling my body that it was strong, and we were going to walk to wherever we were headed, letting no doubt enter my head. It works! It works unbelievably well.

I would also sometimes tell my tennis players to repeat over and over "I'm a great tennis player." Many players thought it silly, but it works, and it works with anything. Whatever it is you want to have happen in your life, tell yourself you will accomplish it. Tell yourself you're beautiful, or smart, or whatever. It will make a difference. Tell yourself every single day for the rest of your life.

I had gained some weight being somewhat sedentary in a wheelchair, but now I had shed much of it and my arms had never been stronger. I was looking for an even tougher challenge. A local marathon was coming up in a few weeks, but it was costly and I didn't really have the extra money to spend. Julie and I went to have a beer at a German bar called the Bier Stube. We sat outside in a relatively empty courtyard, but soon it became filled. The staff and volunteers from the very marathon I wanted to enter were having a meeting there. I eventually met a man named Joe. We hit it off right from the start. He was the one in charge of the marathon, and without me saying a word, he offered me a code to enter his race as a VIP and pay nothing. I got this strange feeling that there was a guiding hand out there helping me. The unlikelihood of all this unfolding like it did still baffles me. I entered the race that night.

It was unusually hot and humid on race day. Julie was working, so I was completely on my own. There were three races: a 5k, a half marathon, and full marathon. Thousands of people were lined up in the street. I was excited to do my first marathon. I always wanted to try one before my accident, but got injured before I got the chance. There were around nine hundred in the marathon.

The gun went off and the crowd slowly moved. Sitting in a wheelchair you really have no idea where you're at, you're just following the mass of humanity surrounding you. Soon I was pushing uphill over a bridge and then another mile long hill. Hills are much easier to run up than push a wheelchair. I soon found myself towards the end of the pack, but eventually things leveled off and I was able to catch up and pass some people.

I had to stop three times at port-a-potties throughout the race. The accident always left me needing to go more often than I used to.

It was such a beautiful late summer day. We started in the morning, and as the day wore on it just got hotter and hotter. The people spread out more and more. There were about a hundred people behind me and seven hundred in front. At about twenty miles I had to cross a bridge. My arms ached getting up to the crest and then I let my chair fly down the other side. It took me to where the race originated. It had been complete solitude, and it turned into a cheering multitude. Hundreds of fans cheered at the bottom of the hill, and because I was the only person pushing their own wheelchair in the race, they cheered a little louder. I passed by this cheering crowd with little kids and adults holding their hands out wanting me to give them a high-five, I slapped a few, but you have to realize that my hands were busy pushing my chair so I passed most of them with only a fatigued smile.

Crossing the finish line at the Quad Cities Marathon.

The finish line was only a matter of yards away, but the cruel irony of the moment was that all marathoners still had to go down the road three miles and come back to get the twenty-six miles in. The last three miles were the toughest as my left leg started to spasm. I couldn't keep it on my footrest and finished the last three miles with my legs crossed. I would often get spasms when my body was in distress, and this was no exception. Joe brought out a ribbon at the finishing line and let me plow through it. I said right after the race that I'd never do another marathon again, but I have since done another half marathon and am looking forward to many more marathons in the future.

I can honestly say I'm a very happy person. I still yearn occasionally for some of the things lost, but I look around me and see people blindly going through life miserable. Having all the power to make a positive change in their lives, but being bound by acquiring money or materials. They are too afraid or insecure to go outside their comfort zone and give up what they've become accustomed to, and that is tearing them down.

So many of us are creatures of habit. When life travels down a path that wasn't meant for us, we'd rather follow the course than take a chance on a new one. The accident sent me on a completely new course and I see the path more clearly than I did before. I'm not bound to this path and am ready to find another if I need to. Would I have thought this way before my car accident? I have no idea, but does it matter?

Earlier I mentioned that I accept my situation but am not resigned to it. What I meant by that statement is that I am okay with who I am. I accept my strengths and weaknesses. I know that each and every day I can be better tomorrow. I work hard on my arms and legs everyday, harder than I ever worked when I was able-bodied, so I'm not resigned to being locked in to my current condition. I know I can, and will, be better tomorrow if I do what I need to do today.

We can all be better. We may not always go as far as we want, but we can always strive to go farther than we have before. It's not limited to just the physical. We can all make an effort to improve mentally, emotionally and spiritually. That might even be just accepting that your time on Earth is over.

I don't believe we ever stay the same, because when we fail to strive to improve we regress. One day is never quite the same as the next. You have a choice to climb that next hill, but don't worry if you don't reach its peak. Take time to turn around and stare at the path you took.

My doctor told me over twenty years ago that my improvements would end after about a month, and here I am, still improving. Never let anyone tell you what you can or can't do! You make the choices that determine the path you're on, and where that path will take you.

I no longer need to dream to feel free. I have learned the most precious lesson. Life is truly from the shoulders up. I would love to regain all of the abilities that were taken away from me that fateful day, but life goes on, and you do the best that you can with what you've got. Don't dwell on all the things that are lacking in your life, but instead, cherish all the wonderful things you have. I know I do.

I am now twenty-two years out from my accident and feel I'm still improving. I came across my doctor who did the surgery on me so long ago. We were sitting next to each other when he recognized me. I eventually showed him the progress I had made by holding his wife's hand and walking across the room. I could see in his face he was deeply moved. He had told my mother that he'd have a better chance of winning the lottery than me ever walking again. If my mother were still alive she would have loved to see this moment. Who knows? Maybe she did.

I told him how fortunate I was to get to this point in my recovery. He looked me in the eye and said it was all the work I've done over the years that got me to where I am. I thought about it for a moment, and I think about everything that went into it. It was all part of the journey. I am thankful for all of it.

It's been over twenty years since that life shattering moment. You'd think by now I'd incorporate my disability into my dreams at night, but it's never happened. I can walk and get around just the way I used to. I still run in my dreams.

Made in the USA
Charleston, SC
21 February 2016